Le Poulet Rouge Restaurant

Cookbook

Tim Holley

Rosie! Hope you enjoy the book. Here's cooking at you. Best Wishes

Tim

For information call: Sunnyside Up Productions
                          P.O. Box 425
                          Boise ID 83701
                          (208) 343-2993

Library of Congress Catalog Number: 96-79344
International Standard Book Number: 1-887747-02-8
First Printing: November, 1996
Printed and bound in United States of America

Edited by: Jean Terra, Erin Stoops and Romaine Galey Hon
Design and Layout: Cathy Venosdel
Printed by Northwest Printing, Boise, Idaho

Published by: Legendary Publishing
                                    Lorry Roberts, Publisher
                                    P.O. Box 7706
                                    Boise ID 83707-1706

This book is available at special discounts for bulk purchases for
sales promotions, premiums and for fund-raising. For details,
contact Legendary Publishing by telephone at 800-358-1929

This book is dedicated to my son, Max,
who has added the perfect amount of
spice and seasoning to my life.

ACKNOWLEDGMENTS

Many people were involved in the production of this book and I am truly grateful to each and every one of them. I especially want to thank:

Lorry Roberts, my publisher, who helped me from the very beginning, supplying me with information, advice and friendship.

Cathy Venosdel of Typestyle, Inc. for her invaluable skills and expertise. I took a construction paper "mockup" of my book to Cathy and supplied her with recipes. From that, she formatted the design and layout.

Both Lorry and Cathy have made the publication of my first book not only a memorable but a pleasurable experience.

A very special thank you to my sisters who have helped me so much both personally and professionally; Jeanne helped with the typing and editing of most of the recipes and Sandy helped with the design and marketing of the book.

My sincere thanks also to:

Erin Stoops, a great Le Poulet Rouge cook, who helped with the development of recipes and the edit and design of the book.

Romaine Hon, who helped revise and edit the recipes and who provided me with her valuable professional advice, for which I am most appreciative.

Jean Terra, who edited and revised all parts of this book, for her expertise and advice but, mostly, for her patience.

Cynthia Sandoval, for her help in revising, writing, and testing the desserts and baked goods recipes. Also for her support and friendship.

Lisa Cherkasky, my friend and mentor, as well as the best cook I've ever worked with, for her help and guidance.

Governor Cecil Andrus for his support and kind remarks and Clareene Wharry for her assistance.

Senator Dirk Kempthorne for his patronage and support.

L'Academie de Cuisine and especially Patrice Dionot for all their help.

Phylis King, for her excellent photography skills.

Everyone at Typestyle, Inc.

Special thanks to the following people for their support and friendship: John Clohessy, Sus and Fred Helpenstell, Kathy McCormick, Tom O'Connor, Barbara Krogh, Barbara MacGregor, Connie Hassan, Marla Kober Upham, Joan Carley, Dave Emberton, Mark "Jazmo" Seiler and Rebecca Stone, Jerry Carter, Rodney Valentine, Stephanie Burgess, Mary Ryder, George and Marguerite Emerson, Lyn Marchend, Steve and Linda Swanson, Wallace Yates, Richard and Judy Steele, Nancy Ward, Patrick L. Hughes, Larry and Jill Costello, Rebecca Robinson, Callie Sands, Bette Stevens, Paula Pitt, Katharine Gerrity, Virginia Moore, Chris Binion, John Roberts, Paddy Yancey, Fred Norman, Jean Smith, Dave and Shiela Mills, Jim and Mary Quinn, Mr. and Mrs. James J. Coughlin, John and Mikel Ward, Pat Nelson, Al and Berit Kuykendall, Mike and Debra Crisler. An extra note of thanks to Berit and Debra for all their input, encouragement and support. And a very special thank you to Vicki Nucci, who purchased the first book.

Le Poulet Rouge restaurant, located in the heart of downtown Boise, Idaho, near the corner of 6th and Main Streets, has been serving breakfast, lunch, baked goods and desserts for over 12 years.

All food at Le Poulet Rouge is prepared fresh daily in limited quantities, just enough to serve one day's meals. Cooks and bakers work in an open-style kitchen that allows our customers to watch their food being prepared.

Our menu changes constantly except for some Le Poulet Rouge "signature" items. Food is displayed in a glassfront case at the point where customers form a line to order. By making selections from the soups, salads, sandwiches, quiches, entrees and pastries on display, customers can create their own made-to-order breakfast or lunch. We try to have the food ready by the time the customer is seated. When a particular food item is sold out, it is removed from the display.

The concept for Le Poulet Rouge was originally developed by Chris Binion and Rory Farrow. By serving unique and exciting food in a Bistro-type atmosphere, they developed a loyal clientele that has lasted to this day.

Rory eventually sold her half of the partnership to John Roberts. Under the direction of Chris Binion and John Roberts, I worked as Head Chef of Le Poulet Rouge for three years, cooking and creating recipes and menus. John and Chris then sold the restaurant to me and my wife Amy Holley.

After contemplating writing a cookbook for years, I finally decided the time had come to share some of our favorite recipes with friends of Le Poulet Rouge who have supported us for years. On May 1, 1996, in order to make it possible for me to concentrate on the creation of this book, Amy and I sold Le Poulet Rouge to RaDawn Anthony and John Smythe. I continue to serve as Head Chef.

This book has been made possible by the collaboration of effort. Recipes have been contributed from several sources. Some of the people responsible for recipe development and preparation are Chris Binion, Rory Farrow, Marguerite Shank, Cynthia Sandoval, Dina Krogh, John Clohessy, Kate Barnet, Karen Dooley, Berit Kuykendall, Paddy Yancey, Erin Stoops, Cynthia Hutchinson, Amy Holley, and RaDawn Anthony. They and dozens of others contributed ideas and suggestions and served as "taste-testers."

One thing that has remained constant throughout the several changes of ownership and one change of location for Le Poulet Rouge, is our collective commitment to serving great food at reasonable prices in a comfortable setting. Through the publication of this cookbook, we are pleased to share some of our favorite dishes with you. Bon appétit!

Tim Holley
November, 1996

Blueberry Pancakes with Lemon Ricotta Topping

3 3/4 cups all-purpose flour
1/2 cup sugar
4 tablespoons baking powder
2 teaspoons salt
2 teaspoons cinnamon
1 cup blueberries
6 eggs
15 tablespoons butter, melted (1 cup less 1 tablespoon)

Lemon Ricotta Topping

2 cups ricotta cheese
1/2 cup sugar
2 lemons, zested, juiced

1. Mix all Lemon Ricotta Topping ingredients well. Add more sugar if a sweeter topping is desired. Serve at room temperature on pancakes. This topping can also be used to fill blintzes and crêpes. Reserve.

2. Combine all dry ingredients in mixing bowl.

3. Mix eggs, butter, milk and vanilla in separate bowl.

4. Add egg mixture to dry ingredients. Mix well. Let mixture rest at least 15 minutes.

5. Pour pancake batter onto griddle or skillet.

6. Place 5 to 6 whole blueberries on each pancake. Cook until bubbles begin to appear, then flip pancake and continue to cook approximately 1 1/2 to 2 minutes, or until golden brown. Test center for doneness.

7. Serve with Lemon Ricotta Topping.

(Yield: 8 to 10 servings)

Quiche

Quiche is one of our most popular dishes served at Le Poulet Rouge. We bake 3 to 4 daily, sometimes as many at 8 to 10. This recipe is written for one whole quiche, approximately 9 inches in diameter.

Best described as "egg-pie," quiche can be assembled using a variety of fillings, with a standard egg "custard" poured over the top.

Here are some hints and directions in assembling and baking quiche. The custard, filling suggestions and crust recipes follow.

Hints

- Always bake in a preheated oven at 325 degrees.

- Roll out quiche shell, place in pan and keep in freezer until ready to assemble.

- Have custard prepared and all filling ingredients ready before assembling.

- Most filling ingredients should be cooked before assembly. Vegetables should be blanched, meats cooked, onions sautéed, etc.

   The exception is soft vegetables such as tomatoes, artichoke hearts, or thawed, frozen vegetables such as peas or corn.

- Always place a layer of grated cheese on the bottom of your quiche shell. This will help seal any holes that may occur.

- If you choose to use a variety of cheeses, be sure to place Cheddar cheese on bottom layer, not on the top, as Cheddar browns faster than white cheese such as Monterey Jack, Mozzarella or Swiss.

- Quiche may need to be covered with aluminum foil near end of cooking time if top of quiche is starting to brown.

- To test for doneness: insert a small knife in center of quiche; it should come out "dry." Also, give quiche a gentle shake; it is done when it still jiggles but is firm to the touch.

- Do not slam oven door as this may cause quiche to fall.

Egg Custard

The standard custard we use is as follows:

5 whole eggs
2 tablespoons flour
2 teaspoons salt
1 teaspoon pepper
2 cups heavy whipping cream

1. Mix eggs, flour, salt and pepper. Mixture will appear curdled. Try to break up any flour lumps that may occur.

2. Add heavy cream. Whisk well.

Note: You can add other spices if desired. We add cumin, chile powder, and cayenne pepper for our Mexican-style quiches. This custard works well with all types of quiche.

Filling Suggestions

For quiche assembly, we use approximately:

4 ounces grated cheese for bottom layer
2 to 3 cups filling
4 ounces grated cheese for top layer

Fill the quiche shell with egg custard. If you have excess custard, save and add to eggs for omelettes!

All quiches using this egg custard recipe should serve 8 to 10.

Quiche Crust

3/4 cup unbleached flour
1/3 cup whole wheat flour
1/4 teaspoon salt
6 1/2 tablespoons cold butter, cut up
4 1/2 teaspoons shortening
4 tablespoons ice water

1. In a food processor with metal blade, combine the flours and salt. Add butter and shortening (do not clump together). Toss to coat with flour. Process until mixture resembles fine crumbs. Drizzle ice water over flour and pulse just until dough begins to hold together.

2. Turn dough onto smooth surface and gather into ball. Flatten into a disk. Wrap well with plastic film. Refrigerate 1 hour or overnight.

3. On a lightly floured surface, roll out pastry disk to 1-inch larger than pan diameter. Fold in half and ease into quiche pan. Drop and settle the sides into lower pan edge, mending tears and holes to avoid leakage.

(Yield: Makes single crust)

Mushroom Artichoke Quiche

Layer

Grated cheese (Monterey Jack or Swiss)
Sautéed leeks
Sautéed mushrooms
Artichoke hearts, chopped
Green onions, chopped
Fresh basil, chopped
Grated cheese

Bacon Tomato Quiche

Layer

Grated Cheddar cheese
Sliced fresh Roma tomatoes
Sautéed bacon and onions
Grated Monterey Jack cheese

Crab and Artichoke

Layer

Grated white cheese
Frozen spinach, squeezed dry
Fresh tomatoes, sliced
Fresh crab meat
Artichoke hearts, chopped
Parmesan cheese
Salt and pepper
Grated white cheese

Denver Quiche

6 ounces ham, cubed, cooked
1/2 yellow onion, chopped
1 red bell pepper, diced
1 green bell pepper, diced

1. Sauté onions and bell peppers until tender. Add ham and salt and pepper.

2. Layer

   Grated Cheddar cheese
   Ham and pepper mixture
   Grated Monterey Jack cheese

Garden Quiche

2 garlic cloves, chopped
1/2 medium yellow onion, diced
1 red bell pepper, diced
1 green bell pepper, diced
1 zucchini, thinly sliced
1 carrot, peeled, diced small
1 Idaho potato, peeled, cubed in 1/2-inch pieces
1/3 cup frozen peas, thawed
1/3 cup frozen corn, thawed
1 tomato, sliced
Salt and pepper
1 teaspoon dried thyme
Fresh basil (optional)

1. Sauté onions and peppers until soft. Add thyme, zucchini, carrot and potato. Cook until vegetables are tender. Remove from heat, add peas, corn, salt and pepper. Mix well. Cool.

2. Layer

   Grated Cheddar cheese
   Vegetable mixture (add basil here if desired)
   Grated Monterey Jack cheese

Chile Relleno Quiche with Ranchero Sauce

Custard

5 eggs
2 cups heavy cream
2 teaspoons ground cumin
2 teaspoons chili powder
2 teaspoons salt
Dash cayenne pepper
2 tablespoons flour

1. Mix custard ingredients well.

2. Layer

    Grated Monterey Jack cheese
    Green chilies, canned, whole, split open
    Grated Cheddar cheese
    Green chilies, as above
    Grated Monterey Jack cheese

3. Pour custard over. Bake. When serving, top with Ranchero Sauce and sour cream.

Ranchero Sauce

1 medium yellow onion, diced
4 garlic cloves, chopped
2 tablespoons chili powder
2 tablespoons ground cumin
2 teaspoons salt
1 teaspoon black pepper
1 teaspoon red pepper flakes
2 28-ounce cans tomatoes, chopped

Sauté onions, garlic and all spices. Add tomatoes and simmer
30 to 45 minutes.

Mexican Scrambled Eggs

2 tablespoons olive oil
1 red bell pepper, diced
1 jalapeño, halved, seeded, chopped fine
1/2 cup green onion, sliced thin
4 corn tortillas, cut in strips, then cut in half
12 eggs, beaten
1/4 cup Monterey Jack cheese, grated
1/4 cup Cheddar cheese, grated
Salt, freshly-ground pepper to taste

1. Sauté red pepper and jalapeño in oil until tender, approximately 5 minutes.

2. Add green onions and tortilla strips, cook 1 minute.

3. Add eggs, salt and pepper. Cook eggs 2 to 3 minutes or until lightly scrambled.

4. Add grated cheeses and fold into eggs to melt.

5. Serve with salsa.

(Yield: 6 to 8 servings)

Breakfast Tostada

1 recipe Mexican Scrambled Eggs (preceding page)
6 corn tortillas
12 tomato slices
1 cup refried beans, warmed (may use canned)
1/2 cup Cheddar cheese, grated
1/2 cup Monterey Jack cheese, grated

1. Cook tortillas in olive oil, 1 at a time, until lightly crisp. Remove from pan. Place on paper towels to absorb excess oil. Repeat until 6 shells are prepared. Keep warm.

2. Spread warm refried beans over the tortilla shells.

3. Top each tortilla with 2 tomato slices and grated cheeses (approximately 2 tablespoons of each).

4. Place in 350 degree oven to melt cheese, approximately 3 to 5 minutes.

5. When hot, top each tortilla with Mexican Scrambled Eggs.

6. Garnish with grated cheese, salsa and sour cream.

(Yield: 6 servings)

Crêpes

This recipe makes approximately 18 to 20 crêpes approximately 5 1/2 to 6-inches in diameter.

We use a processor to blend the batter but it can be prepared in a large bowl, making sure to whisk well, trying to eliminate all lumps. Have all ingredients ready.

1/4 granulated sugar
1 cup flour
2/3 cup whole milk
2/3 cup water
3 large eggs
1/4 teaspoon salt
3 tablespoons butter, melted, or vegetable oil
1 tablespoon vanilla

1. Place sugar, flour and salt in processor or bowl and mix well.

2. With processor running, add milk, water, butter (or oil) and vanilla.

3. Add eggs. Combine well. Be sure to scrape the sides of the processor bowl. Process approximately 1 minute until batter is very smooth.

4. Let batter rest at least 1 hour or overnight.

To Cook Crêpes:

Have ready

Crêpe or omelette pan (5 1/2 to 6 inches in diameter)
    make sure pan is spotlessly clean
Melted butter
Prepared crêpe batter
Rubber spatula (do not use metal on a non-stick surface)

1. Heat pan until drops of water sizzle on the surface.

2. Pour approximately 2 tablespoons melted butter in pan, coat well and pour excess butter back and reserve (pan will need to be coated with butter at all times to keep crêpes from sticking).

3. Add approximately 3 tablespoons crêpe batter to pan, turning the pan in all directions, spreading the batter evenly on the bottom pan. (If you have excess batter, pour back into reserved batter.)

4. Cook 30 seconds or so, until lightly browned (lift edge of crêpe with spatula to check brownness).

5. Turn crêpe over and cook 10 to 15 seconds. Remove from pan onto wax paper. Repeat process until all batter is cooked.

Hint

You may need to actually bang the pan on a flat surface to help the crêpe loosen from the bottom of the pan. Also, the best looking side of the crêpe is the side to have facing out.

When cooled, crêpes can be stacked between layers of waxed paper, wrapped and kept in the refrigerator for 2 to 3 days. Crêpes may also be wrapped in aluminum foil and frozen. They are best, however, when used fresh.

Erin's Blintzes

Blintzes are simply filled and folded crêpes, sautéed in butter.

Prepared crêpes (previous recipe)
Sautéed Apples (recipe follows)
Whiskey Sauce (refer to Apple Bread Pudding recipe)

Cheese Filling

1 pound (2 cups) cream cheese, softened
1 cup sugar
1 cup pecans, chopped
2 teaspoons vanilla
2 teaspoons triple sec
2 teaspoons cinnamon

1. Combine all of the filling ingredients, stirring until smooth and well-blended.

2. Place 1 crêpe on work surface, spoon approximately 2 table-spoons of the filling in the center.

3. Fold into small packages. Place the crêpe seam side down on a small sheet, tray or platter. Repeat filling and folding the remaining crêpes (unused crêpes can be frozen and kept for another use).

Sautéed Apples for Topping

3 Granny Smith apples, thinly sliced
3 tablespoons whole butter
3 tablespoons maple syrup
1/4 cup brown sugar
2 teaspoons cinnamon

1. Place butter, brown sugar and cinnamon in skillet. Mix well when butter melts.

2. Add apples to skillet with sugar mixture. Heat until apples are tender, approximately 3 to 5 minutes. Mix well to coat apples. Reserve. Keep warm.

To Serve Blintzes

1. In a large skillet over medium heat, melt 2 tablespoons butter. Cook the blintzes in batches, until lightly browned on both sides, approximately 1 to 1 1/2 minutes per side.

2. Remove blintzes from skillet and keep warm until all blintzes are cooked, adding more butter if necessary.

3. Dust blintzes with powdered sugar.

4. Serve with sautéed apples, drizzle Whiskey Sauce over top.

(Yield: 6 to 8 servings)

Any fruit topping of your choice can be substituted.

Chris and John's Favorite Pancakes

1 cup coconut, shredded
1 cup whole wheat flour
1 1/4 cups all purpose flour
2 cups rolled oats, old fashioned
1 cup brown sugar
2 tablespoons baking powder
2 teaspoons salt
1 cup nuts (chopped pecans, walnuts or sunflower seeds)
2 tablespoons vegetable or canola oil
4 cups milk
2 eggs
2 teaspoons vanilla extract

1. Combine coconut, flours, oats, brown sugar, baking powder, salt and nuts in a mixing bowl.

2. Mix oil, milk, eggs and vanilla in separate bowl.

3. Pour oil mixture into dry ingredients in two parts, mixing well after each addition.

4. Allow batter to sit at least 15 minutes. If batter becomes too thick, add milk to thin batter to desired consistency.

5. Serve with warm maple syrup and applesauce.

(Yield: 6 to 8 servings)

Cornmeal Pancakes with Bacon and Pecans

1/2 cup whole wheat flour
1/2 cup all-purpose flour
1 cup cornmeal
2 teaspoons baking powder
1/2 teaspoon baking soda
1/2 teaspoon salt
1/4 cup brown sugar
1/4 cup granulated sugar
1/2 cup chopped pecans (or walnuts)
1/2 cup bacon, cooked, chopped
2 eggs
1 1/2 cups buttermilk
1/2 cup vegetable or canola oil

1. Combine first 10 ingredients in large bowl.

2. Mix eggs, buttermilk and oil in separate bowl.

3. Add egg mixture to dry ingredients in two batches, beating well after each addition. Allow batter to rest at least 1/2 hour.

(Yield: 6 servings)

Stuffed French Toast

For Custard

4 large eggs
2 cups whole milk
1 cup heavy whipping cream
1 1/2 teaspoons ground cinnamon
1 1/2 teaspoons ground nutmeg
1/4 cup vanilla
1/4 cup brown sugar
1/2 cup granulated sugar
1/4 cup brandy, reserved from filling recipe which follows
12 slices of French bread, sliced 2 inches thick, with a pocket cut
    in the middle (enough to hold 2 to 3 tablespoons)
1/2 cup butter, softened
1/2 cup powdered sugar

For Filling

1/2 cup dried cherries
1/2 cup dried cranberries
2/3 cup brandy, optional
1/2 cup sugar
1 cup toasted walnuts
1 tablespoon orange zest
3 cups cream cheese (3 8-ounce packages)

1. Soak cherries and cranberries in brandy for 30 minutes.

2. After soaking, drain and reserve brandy.

3. Add 1/4 cup brandy to custard mixture (the excess, of course, is
   for the cook!)

4. Place strained cherries, cranberries and all other ingredients in a
   food processor. Combine well, making sure to scrape the sides
   of the processor bowl. More sugar can be added if a sweeter
   filling is desired. This can be made up to week in advance and
   refrigerated until needed.

To Assemble

One key to this recipe is to make sure you have all ingredients and equipment ready before beginning this dish.

1. Preheat oven to 300 degrees. Make sure the cream cheese filling is soft (room temperature).

2. Using spoons, or by filling a pastry bag with no tip, fill each slice of bread. Be sure to completely fill pocket (approximately 3 tablespoons), but do not overfill pocket.

3. Fill all slices of bread. Any extra filling can be reserved for future use (will keep up to one week).

4. Have custard mixture ready. Place bread into the bowl of custard mixture and allow to soak evenly on both sides (do not oversoak).

5. Place 1 teaspoon butter in skillet over medium to low heat. Add 2 slices of bread and cook until each side turns golden brown. Remove from pan and place on a cookie sheet. Reserve. Continue with remaining bread.

(Yield: 6 to 8 servings)

Raisin Cinnamon French Toast

4 large eggs
2 cups whole milk
1 cup heavy whipping cream
1 1/2 teaspoons ground cinnamon
1 1/2 teaspoons ground nutmeg
1/4 cup vanilla extract
1/4 cup brown sugar
1/2 cup granulated sugar
1 loaf raisin bread, sliced (16 slices)
1/2 cup butter, softened
1/2 cup powdered sugar

1. Combine eggs, milk, cream, cinnamon, nutmeg, vanilla and sugars, stirring well to blend.

2. Place bread in bowl with custard mixture and allow to soak evenly on both sides.

3. Place 1 teaspoon butter into heated skillet over medium heat. Add 2 slices of bread, cook until each side turns golden brown. Remove from pan, reserve. Continue with remaining bread.

4. When all bread has been cooked, place on tray or counter. Dust well with powdered sugar through a sifter or fine strainer.

5. Cut each slice in half on the diagonal. Serve warm with maple syrup, or any topping of your choice.

(Yield: 8 servings)

Note

At Le Poulet Rouge, we use a whole wheat raisin walnut bread from Great Harvest Bread, a local bakery featuring a wonderful selection of breads. Any good quality dense raisin bread will do.

Banana Pecan Layer Cake

1 1/2 cup pecans
3 cups unbleached flour
1 teaspoon baking soda
1 teaspoon salt
1 teaspoon cinnamon
1/4 teaspoon freshly grated nutmeg
2 cups sugar
1 1/2 cups canola oil
3 large eggs, beaten
1 8-ounce can crushed pineapple, with liquid
2 cups mashed banana (4 to 6 bananas)
1 1/2 teaspoons vanilla

1. Preheat oven to 350 degrees. Spread pecans on small baking sheet. Bake 8 to 10 minutes or until lightly browned and fragrant. Cool, then chop. Grease and flour two 8 to 9-inch round cake or springform pans.

2. Sift together flour, baking soda, salt, spices and sugar into large bowl. Mix well, set aside.

3. Whisk together oil, eggs and vanilla. Then add bananas, then pineapple, beating well after each addition.

4. Add to flour mixture until just combined. Fold in pecans.

5. Pour into prepared pans.

6. Bake 35 to 50 minutes or until tester inserted in center comes out clean. Cool in pans for 10 minutes. Unmold onto wire racks and cool completely. Fill and frost with Cream Cheese Icing.

(Yield: 12-14 servings)

Italian Cream Layer Cake

1 cup pecans
2/3 cup coconut, unsweetened, shredded
2 1/2 cups unbleached flour
1 teaspoon salt
1/4 teaspoon nutmeg, freshly grated
1/2 cup (1 stick) butter, room temperature
1/2 cup shortening
2 cups sugar
5 eggs, separated
1 cup buttermilk
1 teaspoon vanilla

1. Preheat oven to 350 degrees. Spread pecans on small baking sheet. Bake 8 to 10 minutes or until lightly browned and fragrant. Repeat process with coconut, baking 6 to 8 minutes. Cool. Finely chop pecans. Grease and flour two 2" cake or springform pans.

2. Sift together flour, soda, salt and nutmeg into medium bowl. Set aside.

3. In bowl of large electric mixer cream butter, shortening and sugar until light and fluffy. Add the yolks gradually. Beat well. Scrape down sides of bowl 2 to 3 times during mixing.

4. Stir buttermilk and vanilla together in separate container. In thirds, beginning and ending with the flour mixture, alternately add flour mixture and buttermilk mixture to creamed butter mixture. Blend well after each addition. Scrape down sides of bowl 2 to 3 times during mixing.

5. Stir in pecans and coconut.

6. In another mixer bowl beat the egg whites just to firm peaks. Fold into cake batter. Pour into prepared pans.

7. Bake 25 to 30 minutes, until cake tester inserted in center comes out clean. Cool in pans for 10 minutes. Unmold onto wire racks and cool completely. Fill and frost with Cream Cheese Icing.

(Yield: 12-14 servings)

Nut Bars

1 cup powdered sugar
3 cups unbleached flour
1 1/2 cups (3 sticks) butter, room temperature
1 cup melted butter
1 cup corn syrup
3/4 cup cream
1 cup brown sugar
5 1/2 cups walnuts

1. Preheat oven to 350 degrees. Grease a 15-inch by 10-inch by 1-inch baking sheet or jelly roll pan.

2. In a food processor, combine sugar and flour. Blend about 5 seconds. Add 1 1/2 cups butter. Process until smooth and comes away from sides of bowl. Should be light and fluffy. Pat and press lightly and evenly into pan. Prick with fork.

3. Bake crust 10 minutes or until light golden. Meanwhile, whisk together melted butter, corn syrup, cream and brown sugar in large bowl until smooth and thoroughly blended. Stir in walnuts.

4. Pour walnut mixture over hot crust and gently spread evenly to completely cover crust.

5. Return to oven and bake 20 to 25 minutes until the middle is bubbling, being careful not to overbrown the edges. Cool to room temperature. Press knife into bars to cut.

(Yield: 24 2-inch bars)

Ginger Oatmeal Cookies

1 1/2 cup unbleached flour
2 teaspoons soda
1/2 teaspoon salt
1 teaspoon cinnamon
3/4 teaspoon ground cloves
3/4 teaspoon ground ginger
3/4 cup butter, room temperature
1 cup sugar
1 large egg
1/4 cup molasses
1 tablespoon fresh ginger, minced or grated
2 cups rolled oats, quick cooking
Raw sugar

1. Preheat oven to 350 degrees. Lightly grease cookie sheets or line with baking paper.

2. Sift together flour, soda, salt and spices. Set aside.

3. In bowl of electric mixer, cream together butter and sugar. Beat in egg, ginger and molasses. Scrape bowl sides at least once. Beat well.

4. Stir in flour mixture until blended. Stir in oats until blended. Drop by rounded tablespoon on baking sheets about 2 inches apart.

5. Bake 8 to 10 minutes until browned.

(Yield: About 2 dozen)

Max's Favorite Chocolate Cookies

2 ounces (2 squares) unsweetened chocolate
6 ounces (1 cup) semi-sweet chocolate chips
3 ounces (6 tablespoons) butter
1/4 cup plus 1 tablespoon unbleached flour
1/4 teaspoon baking powder
1/3 teaspoon salt
2 large eggs
3/4 cup sugar
2 tablespoons espresso
1 1/2 teaspoons vanilla
6 ounces (1 cup) semi-sweet chocolate chips
1/2 cup walnuts, chopped
1/2 cup pecans, chopped (toasted is nice)

1. Melt together chocolate squares, 1 cup chocolate chips and butter. Microwave at medium (50%) power for 1 to 3 minutes, stirring each minute until chocolate begins to melt (mixture may also be melted in top of double boiler or over very low heat on stovetop). With a small whisk, blend until smooth. Set aside.

2. Into a small bowl sift the flour, baking powder and salt. Set aside.

3. In a large bowl with electric mixer, combine eggs, sugar, espresso and vanilla, and beat at high speed 1 to 2 minutes. Gradually add melted chocolate at low speed. Scrape bowl. Add flour mixture. Beat at low speed just to mix. Scrape bowl. Fold in 1 cup chocolate chips and nuts.

4. Refrigerate 6 hours to overnight (may be refrigerated up to 3 days). Preheat oven to 350 degrees. Line baking sheet with baking paper (parchment paper). Scoop out 1-inch blobs and place an inch apart on baking sheets. Bake 10 minutes. Cool completely before removing.

(Yield: 6 dozen small cookies)

Mocha Toffee Bars

1 cup butter, room temperature
1 cup firmly packed brown sugar
1 large egg yolk
1 1/2 teaspoons vanilla
3 tablespoons strong espresso, room temperature
2 cups unbleached flour
Semi-sweet chocolate chips
1 cup cashews

1. Preheat oven to 350 degrees. Spread cashews on a small baking sheet. Bake 8 to 10 minutes or until golden and fragrant. Cool.

2. Grease a 15 1/2-inch by10 1/2-inch by 1-inch baking sheet or jelly roll pan.

3. In bowl of electric mixer, cream butter and brown sugar until light and fluffy. Beat in egg yolk. Combine espresso and vanilla and beat into butter mixture a little at a time. Beat well and scrape down sides of bowl once during mixing.

4. Add flour. Mix well, scraping sides of bowl 1 to 2 times during mixing. Spoon dollops of batter around edge of pan, then spread to fill pan.

5. Bake 15 to 20 minutes, or until crust pulls away slightly from pan edge. Immediately remove from the oven and sprinkle chocolate chips on the crust and let cool 15 to 20 minutes. Gently spread the melted chocolate over crust. Sprinkle the cashews on the chocolate and lightly press.

6. Cool to room temperature or until chocolate is firm but not hard. Cut into squares.

(Yield: 24 2-inch bars)

Lemon Poppyseed Muffins

2 lemons, zested, juiced
Milk, combined with above lemon juice to make 1 cup liquid
1/2 cup sour cream
2 large eggs
1 teaspoon vanilla
3 1/2 cups unbleached flour
1 cup sugar
1 1/2 tablespoons baking powder
1/2 teaspoon salt
1/4 cup poppy seeds
3/4 cup (1 1/2 sticks) cold butter

Lemon Glaze

1 lemon, juiced
1 tablespoon orange juice
Generous 1/3 cup powdered sugar

1. Preheat oven to 375 degrees. Grease muffin tin. Spray well with pan coating.

2. Whisk together Lemon Glaze ingredients in small bowl. Reserve.

3. In a medium bowl, whisk together milk, juice, sour cream, vanilla and eggs. Set aside.

4. Sift together flour, baking soda, salt and sugar into a large bowl. Mix well. Cut in butter until pea-sized pieces form. Sprinkle in poppy seeds and toss to mix.

5. Add the liquid mixture to the flour mixture, stirring until just blended.

6. Spoon into muffin tins, filling each cup 3/4 fill. Bake 20 to 30 minutes until toothpick inserted in muffin center comes out clean. Brush with Lemon Glaze. Cool in tins 5 minutes, then remove to wire rack to finish cooling.

(Yield: 12 muffins)

Whole Wheat Bread with Walnuts and Raisins

1 envelope plus 1 teaspoon dry yeast
Pinch of sugar
3 cups warm water
4 cups unbleached all-purpose flour
1 tablespoon salt
2 cups whole wheat flour
1 cup rye flour
1/2 cup Bran Buds or All-Bran
1 cup raisins
1 cup walnuts or pecans, coarsely chopped

1. Mix yeast, sugar, 2 cups all-purpose flour, whole wheat flour and rye flours and salt into mixer bowl of heavy duty mixer. Using paddle attachment, mix at low speed until all are combined. Pour in warm water while mixer is running and beat at medium speed for 5 minutes.

2. Attach dough hook to mixer. Add Bran Buds and knead for 5 minutes, adding the remaining all-purpose flour.

3. Turn the dough out on a lightly-floured surface and knead 2 to 3 minutes. Oil a large bowl; add the dough and turn to coat with oil. Cover with plastic wrap and let rise for 1 1/2 hours. (If you are not ready for the final forming, punch the dough down and let it rise again. This actually improves the flavor, especially if you have used a fast acting yeast.)

4. Punch dough down, knead in raisins and walnuts. Cut dough in half and shape into to oblong or round balls. Smooth by stretching dough out, then tucking dough under. Dust the backs of two cookie sheets with cornmeal. Place the formed loaves into large loaf pans (5-inch by 9-inch). Cover and let rise about an hour until double in size.

5. Preheat oven to 475 degrees. Set a jelly roll pan or metal cake pan on oven floor or lowest rack. Using a fine sifter, dust the top of the loaves with flour. Cut a crisscross pattern in the top of dough.

6. Slide the loaves onto baking stones or place the pans
   directly into the oven. At the same time pour 1 1/2 cups
   hot water into the jelly roll pan and close the oven door
   immediately to trap the steam. Every 2 or 3 minutes, mist the bread
   and sides of the oven with water using a spray bottle with a fine
   spray. Bake for 8 minutes. Reduce heat to 375 degrees and continue
   baking for 35 to 40 minutes or until the bottom sounds hollow when
   tapped. If baking on the pans, turn bread over and bake another
   5 minutes. Cool bread on rack.

(Yield: 2 loaves)

Hint

Can be used for French toast.

Desserts & Pastries

Fruit and Nut Oatmeal Muffins

1 orange, zested, juiced
Milk, combined with above orange juice to make 2 cups
2 cups oatmeal, quick cooking
2 cups unbleached flour
3 teaspoons baking soda
3 teaspoons baking powder
1 cup (2 sticks) butter, melted
2 large eggs
1 cup brown sugar
1 cup dried fruit of choice, chop if necessary
1 cup nuts of choice, chopped, toasted (optional step)
1 teaspoon cinnamon
1/4 teaspoon nutmeg, freshly grated

1. Preheat oven to 375 degrees. Put paper baking cups in muffin tins. Spray lightly with pan coating.

2. In a small bowl stir together oatmeal and milk mixture. Set aside.

3. Sift together flour, baking soda, baking powder, and spices into large bowl. Set aside.

4. In a medium bowl, whisk together butter, eggs and brown sugar.

5. Add the oatmeal mixture, egg mixture, fruit and nuts to the flour mixture. Stir just until well combined. Spoon into prepared muffin tins, filling each cup 3/4 full. Bake 20 to 30 minutes, until toothpick inserted in muffin center comes out clean. Cool in tins at least 5 minutes (they can be very delicate and crumbly).

(Yield: 10-12 muffins)

Blueberry Scones

3 1/3 cups unbleached flour
3/4 cup sugar
1 tablespoon baking powder
1/2 teaspoon salt
6 ounces butter, cool, cubed
3 large eggs
1/4 cup plus 2 tablespoons cream
1 teaspoon vanilla
1/2 lemon, zested
1 cup frozen blueberries

1. Preheat oven to 350 degrees.

2. In a large bowl, sift together flour, sugar, baking powder and salt. Cut butter into flour mixture until it resembles coarse cornmeal.

3. In a medium bowl, whisk eggs (reserve 2 teaspoons of beaten egg and mix with 2 teaspoons of water to make egg wash. Reserve). Add cream, vanilla and zest to remaining beaten eggs and whisk until well blended.

4. Add egg mixture to flour mixture. Stir with a fork until dough cleans side of bowl. Turn out onto lightly floured smooth surface. Knead very lightly until well combined.

5. Roll and put dough into an 11-inch by 8-inch rectangle, 1/2-inch thick. Evenly distribute frozen berries over dough, leaving a 3/4-inch unfilled strip along long edges. Press berries into dough. Starting on a long side, roll firmly into a cylinder. With long edge seam side down, press roll to 1 1/2-inch thickness. Mark, then cut in a zig-zag manner, into 8 triangles.

6. Place evenly on a large baking sheet lined with baking paper. Brush scones with egg wash. Sprinkle with sugar if desired. Bake 25 to 30 minutes or until tester comes out clean.

(Yield: 8 large scones)

Vanilla Shortbread

1 cup (2 sticks) butter, room temperature
1/2 cup sugar
2 1/2 cups unbleached flour
1 teaspoon vanilla
2 tablespoons sugar

1. Preheat oven to 350 degrees.

2. With an electric mixer in a medium to large bowl, cream butter and sugar until light and fluffy. Scrape bowl occasionally. Beat in vanilla. Stir in the flour and blend well. Should be crumbly.

3. Lightly and evenly press dough into a 9-inch tart pan with removable bottom. Prick well with fork. Sprinkle sugar over dough. Bake 30 to 35 minutes, until pale golden.

4. Cool to slightly warm, remove from pan. Cut in 8 or 10 large wedges.

Chocolate Shortbread

1/2 cup Ghirardelli cocoa powder
2 cups unbleached flour
1 cup (2 sticks) butter, room temperature
1/2 cup sugar
1/2 cup semi-sweet chocolate chips
1 tablespoon sugar

1. Preheat oven to 350 degrees.

2. Sift together the flour and cocoa. Stir and toss to mix. Set aside.

3. With an electric mixer in a medium to large bowl, cream the butter and sugar until light and fluffy. Scrape the bowl several times during beating. Stir in the flour mixture and blend well (mixture should be crumbly).

4. Lightly and evenly press the dough into a 9-inch tart pan with a removable bottom. Prink well with fork. Sprinkle and press in the chocolate chips. Sprinkle sugar over dough. Bake 30 to 35 minutes.

5. Cool to slightly warm. Remove from pan and cut into 8 to 10 large wedges.

Lemon Bars

1 cup (2 sticks) butter, room temperature
1/2 cup powdered sugar, sifted
2 cups unbleached flour
4 large eggs
2 cups sugar
1 lemon, zested
6 tablespoons lemon juice, fresh
1/3 cup unbleached flour
1 teaspoon baking powder
Powdered sugar

1. Preheat oven to 350 degrees. Lightly grease a 9-inch by 13-inch pan.

2. In a medium to large bowl with an electric mixer, cream butter and sugar until light and fluffy. Blend in flour, scraping sides of bowl occasionally.

3. Evenly, and with medium pressure, press the dough into the prepared pan. Bake 20 minutes.

4. Meanwhile, in a medium to large bowl with an electric mixer, beat the eggs until light and frothy. Gradually add the sugar and lemon zest, beating until thick. Add lemon juice, flour and baking powder. Beat until well blended

5. Pour over the hot baked crust, return to oven and bake 15 to 20 minutes or until pale golden. Remove from oven, sift powdered sugar over the bar. Cool in the pan. Cut into 2-inch squares.

(Yield: 24 2-inch bars)

Ophelia's Cookies

4 cups unbleached flour
4 1/2 teaspoons cinnamon
1 tablespoon baking powder
1 cup (2 sticks) butter, room temperature
1 1/2 cups brown sugar
2 large eggs
1 1/2 cups pecans, chopped

1. Sift together flour, cinnamon and baking powder. Stir and toss to mix. Set aside.

2. In a large bowl, cream together butter and brown sugar. Add eggs and beat well. Scrape down sides of bowl a couple of times. Add the flour mixture and stir until combined. Mix in nuts.

3. Shape dough into two 8-inch long, 2-inch diameter squarish rolls. Wrap well in plastic film. Refrigerate 4 hours to 1 week.

4. Preheat oven to 350 degrees. Cut roll into 1/2-inch slices. Place a little apart and evenly on ungreased baking sheet (lined with baking paper works especially well). Bake 10 to 12 minutes (longer if you want them crispy). Cool briefly, then remove to wire rack to cool completely.

(Yield: about 2 1/2 dozen)

Apple Bread Pudding

9 large croissants
1 Granny Smith apple, peeled, cut in large pea-size chunks,
  tossed with 2 tablespoons sugar
5 cups milk
1/2 cup raisins
3 large eggs
1 tablespoon pure vanilla
1 cup sugar
1/2 teaspoon freshly grated nutmeg
Whipped cream, sweetened to taste

Whiskey Sauce

6 tablespoons unsalted butter, melted
1 cup powdered sugar
1 egg
1 to 2 tablespoons sour mash whiskey, or to taste

1. The night before, cut or tear croissants into bite-sized chunks.
   Combine croissant and apple chunks with milk and raisins. Toss to
   distribute ingredients, cover and refrigerate overnight or for at least
   12 hours.

2. Preheat oven to 350 degrees. Combine eggs, vanilla, sugar and
   nutmeg in a small bowl and whisk to combine. Pour custard into
   croissant mixture and mix well. Pour into a buttered 8-inch by 11-inch
   glass baking dish and bake for one hour or until puffy and browned.

3. While pudding is baking prepare Whiskey Sauce. Whisk egg in small
   bowl, slowly adding melted butter. Stir in powdered sugar and
   whiskey and mix well. The sauce may be made a day before, and
   keeps for 2 to 3 days in the refrigerator. Reserve.

4. As soon as pudding is removed from the oven, pour Whiskey
   Sauce over top. Let cool about 5 minutes before serving with
   whipped cream.

Hint

If not using fresh nutmeg, substitute 3/4 teaspoon ground nutmeg.
Freshly grated, however, is infinitely more satisfying.

Desserts & Pastries

Poo-Berry Bars

2 cups unbleached flour
2/3 cup sugar
1 cup (2 sticks) butter, room temperature
3 large eggs
1 cup brown sugar
1 teaspoon vanilla
1/2 teaspoon salt
1 1/2 cups blueberries, frozen
1 1/2 cups walnuts, chopped
1/2 recipe Cream Cheese Icing

1. Preheat oven to 350 degrees. Lightly grease a 9-inch by 13-inch pan.

2. In a medium to large bowl, combine and mix together the flour and sugar. Add butter and blend with an electric mixer, scraping down sides of bowl with a rubber spatula. Mixture should be crumbly. Distribute and press evenly into pan. Bake 10 minutes.

3. Meanwhile, combine in mixer the eggs, brown sugar, vanilla and salt. Beat well. Dust and toss the blueberries with 2 teaspoons of flour. Fold the blueberries and nuts into egg mixture.

4. Pour and spread mixture evenly over hot baked crust. Bake about 25 minutes or until toothpick inserted in the center comes out clean (taking into consideration the cooked blueberries). Cool in pan on wire rack. Frost with Cream Cheese Icing. Cut into 2-inch squares

(Yield: 24 2-inch bars)

Hint

Press knife into bars to cut.

Cream Cheese Icing

8 ounces cream cheese, room temperature
6 tablespoons butter, room temperature
1 orange or lemon, zested
1/2 orange or lemon, juiced
1 1/2 teaspoons vanilla
3 cups powdered sugar, sifted

1. In a large bowl with an electric mixer, beat cream cheese, butter, zest and juice, and vanilla until very light and fluffy. Scrape bowl occasionally.

2. Beat in about one half the powdered sugar, mix well, then add remaining powdered sugar. Beat until light and fluffy (spreading consistency).

(Yield: 2 1/2 cups, enough for 1 cake)

Saturday Brunch Fruit Crisp

1 orange or lemon, zested
1/2 orange or lemon, juiced
1/2 cup brown sugar
1/2 cup tapioca
10 cups fresh or frozen fruit or combination of fruits
    (*Examples:* Apple/blueberry (lemon, toasted almonds);
    Marionberry/blueberry/strawberry (orange, toasted
    hazelnuts); Peach (orange, 1/2 teaspoon minced fresh ginger,
    toasted pecans)
3/4 cup nuts
3/4 cup unbleached flour
1/2 teaspoon nutmeg, grated fresh
1/3 cup sugar
3/4 cup brown sugar
6 ounces (1 1/2 sticks) butter, cold
1 cup oatmeal, quick cooking
Cinnamon sugar

1. Preheat oven to 350 degrees. Grease a 13-inch by 9-inch by 2 1/2-inch pan.

2. In a very large bowl, combine brown sugar and tapioca. Add fruit, juice and zest. Toss to mix. Turn into pan. Level fruit. Sprinkle nuts over.

3. In a medium bowl combine flour, nutmeg, sugar and brown sugar. Cut in butter until mixture resembles crumbs. Stir in oats. Sprinkle evenly over fruit; sprinkle cinnamon sugar over oat mixture. Bake 45 minutes or until top is golden and fruit is bubbly. Serve warm with whipped cream.

(Yield: 8 to 10 servings)

Hint

For cinnamon sugar, mix 3 parts sugar to 1 part cinnamon (example: 9 tablespoons sugar to 3 tablespoons cinnamon). Make as much as you want and store in a spice jar for other uses.

Ginger Carrot Cake

3/4 cup pecans
2 cups unbleached flour
2 teaspoons baking soda
1 1/2 teaspoons cinnamon
1 teaspoon salt
1/2 teaspoon ground ginger
1/2 teaspoon nutmeg, grated fresh
Pinch of ground cloves
1/2 cup (1 stick) butter
1 cup sugar
3/4 cup packed brown sugar
4 large eggs
1 tablespoon fresh ginger, finely minced
1/2 cup canola oil
3 cups grated carrots

1. Preheat oven to 350 degrees. Spread pecans on a small baking sheet. Bake 8 to 10 minutes or until lightly browned and fragrant. Cool, then chop. Grease and flour two 9-inch round cake pans.

2. Sift together flour, baking soda, cinnamon, salt, ground ginger, nutmeg and cloves. Toss and stir to mix. Set aside.

3. In a large bowl with an electric mixer, beat together butter, sugar and brown sugar until light and fluffy. Beat in fresh ginger. Add eggs two at a time, beating well after each addition. Scrape bowl occasionally. Beat 2 minutes more until mixture is light and fluffy. Gradually beat in oil in a thin, steady stream until blended.

4. Add flour mixture to butter mixture. Mix on low speed until just blended. Stir in carrots and pecans. Pour batter into prepared pans.

5. Bake 40 to 45 minutes, or until toothpick inserted in the center comes out clean. Cool cakes in pans 10 minutes, then unmold onto wire racks. Invert again and cool completely. Fill and frost with Cream Cheese Icing (with orange zest). Decorate with toasted pecan halves brushed with warm honey.

(Yield: 12 to 14 servings)

Herb Biscuits

3 cups unbleached flour
1 teaspoon salt
2 tablespoons baking powder
1 tablespoon tarragon or mixed herbs
1/2 cup (1 stick) plus 3 tablespoons butter, chilled
1 3/4 to 2 cups milk

1. Preheat oven to 400 degrees.

2. Into large bowl sift together flour, salt and baking powder. Cut in the butter until size of peas. Add herbs and toss to mix.

3. Add milk all at once. Stir until combined, knead lightly (do not overmix).

4. Roll out to 1-inch thickness on a lightly floured board. Cut into 3-inch to 4-inch rounds. Space evenly on an ungreased baking sheet. Bake 10 to 15 minutes.

(Yield: 8 to 10 biscuits)

Apple Walnut Muffins

1 1/2 cups Granny Smith apples, unpeeled, diced
3/4 cup walnuts, chopped
1 1/2 cups sugar
1 cup plus 2 tablespoons canola oil
3 large eggs
1 1/2 teaspoons vanilla
3 cups unbleached flour
1 1/8 teaspoons baking soda
3/4 teaspoon salt
1 1/4 teaspoons cinnamon

1. Preheat oven to 350 degrees. Grease muffin tin (pan spray works well).

2. Sift together flour, baking soda, salt and cinnamon. Stir and toss. Set aside.

3. In a large bowl with electric mixer, beat together sugar and oil for 2 minutes. Add eggs and vanilla, beat 1 minute.

4. Add and stir the flour mixture into the sugar mixture. Halfway to "just combined," add apples and walnuts. Stir until just combined.

5. Spoon into prepared muffin tin, filling each cup 3/4 to level. Bake 20 to 25 minutes until a toothpick inserted in muffin center comes out clean. Cool in tin at least 3 minutes, then remove to wire rack to cool.

(Yield: 1 dozen large muffins)

Corn Cheddar Muffins

2 cups unbleached flour
4 teaspoons baking powder
1 teaspoon baking soda
1 teaspoon salt
2 tablespoons sugar
2/3 cup cornmeal
1 1/2 cups sour cream
5 eggs
2/3 cup canola oil
2 1/2 cups Cheddar cheese, shredded
1/2 cup green onions, chopped
1/2 teaspoon red pepper flakes

1. Preheat oven to 350 degrees. Grease muffin tins well, including top surfaces of tin.

2. Into a large bowl sift flour, baking powder, soda, salt and sugar. Combine together, then add cornmeal. Mix. Set aside.

3. In a medium bowl whisk together sour cream, eggs and oil. Set aside.

4. In food processor with metal blade, combine cheese, onion and pepper. Pulse 3 to 4 times. Add sour cream mixture and blend. Add this to flour mixture. Stir until just combined.

5. Spoon into prepared muffin tin, filling each cup a generous 3/4 full. Bake 15 to 20 minutes, until golden and toothpick inserted in center comes out clean. Cool briefly in tin; remove to wire rack to finish cooling.

(Yield: 1 dozen muffins)

Brioche Dough

2 teaspoons sugar
1 1/2 tablespoons active dry yeast
1/2 cup (scant) warm water
1 1/2 cups (3 sticks) butter, room temperature
6 eggs, room temperature
4 cups unbleached flour (approximately)
3/4 teaspoon salt

1. In a medium bowl, toss sugar and yeast together. Gently stir in warm water. Set aside.

2. In a large bowl, blend eggs with a dough hook or large spoon. Add salt and butter in small pieces. Blend briefly. Add yeast mixture and 2 cups of flour. Blend for a couple minutes. Add 2 more cups flour. Blend until flour is evenly moistened and dough holds together. Knead until dough is smooth and velvety. If kneading by hand, knead about 5 minutes. If using machine, knead until dough pulls away from bowl sides. For both processes, add flour as needed, up to 3/4 cup.

3. Place dough in a greased bowl, turning over to grease top. Cover and let rise until doubled, about 1 to 2 hours, in a warm place.

4. Punch dough down, pull edges to center. Knead briefly. Return to greased bowl. Cover with plastic wrap and refrigerate overnight.

Sticky Buns

2 tablespoons (2 packages) active dry yeast
1/2 cup warm water
2 cups buttermilk, lukewarm
1 cup (2 sticks) butter, melted
7 cups unbleached flour
1 cup whole wheat flour
1/4 teaspoon baking soda
2 teaspoons salt
1/4 cup sugar
2 large eggs
1/4 cup butter, melted
1/2 cup sugar
1 teaspoon cinnamon
1/2 cup raisins

Topping

3 cups brown sugar
1 1/2 cups (3 sticks) butter, melted
1 3/4 cup cream
2 teaspoons cinnamon
1 cup walnuts

1. In a small bowl, stir together yeast and water. Set aside. In a large bowl (in which kneading will be done) whisk together buttermilk and butter. In another large bowl, combine and toss together flours, baking soda, salt and sugar. Set aside.

2. Add yeast mixture to buttermilk mixture and stir. Add 3/4 of flour mixture and the eggs to the liquid mixture and beat well. Scrape bowl occasionally. Blend in the remaining flour mixture and knead with dough hook 3 to 5 minutes or by hand 5 to 10 minutes until smooth and elastic.

3. Turn over in large greased bowl to grease the top. Cover and let rise in warm place about 1 hour.

4. Meanwhile, in a large bowl, whisk together brown sugar, butter, cream and cinnamon. Grease an 11-inch by 15-inch by 2-inch baking pan. Pour the mixture into pan and spread evenly. Evenly sprinkle walnuts over mixture in pan. Set aside.

5. Punch down dough, pull sides into the center. On a lightly floured surface, shape and roll into a rectangle 1/2-inch thick, 10 inches wide and approximately 18 inches long. Brush with butter, leaving a 1-inch unbuttered border on one of the long sides (this will be a sealed seam). Evenly sprinkle the cinnamon sugar, then raisins, over the dough avoiding the unbuttered border.

6. Starting on the opposite long side, snugly roll into a cylinder. Pinch the seam to seal. Seam side down, mark to cut for 15 rolls. Place pretty side down in prepared pan (3 rolls x 5 rolls). Cover and let rise in warm place until doubled.

7. Meanwhile, preheat oven to 375 degrees. Bake about 25 minutes until lightly browned. While hot, carefully (sauce is very hot) invert onto large baking sheet with sides. Scrape the sauce onto buns. Cool 10 minutes before serving.

Desserts & Pastries

Lemon Mousse

Created by Pastry Chef Dina Krogh, this recipe won "Best Dessert" by a panel of judges at Boise's Annual Riverfest celebration.

3 packages gelatin
2/3 cup warm water
10 eggs, separated
2 cups granulated sugar
1 tablespoon lemon zest, chopped
1 1/4 cups lemon juice
2 1/2 cups heavy whipping cream

1. Combine gelatin and water, let soften while proceeding with recipe.

2. Combine egg yolks, sugar, lemon zest and juice in a heavy-bottomed, stainless steel saucepan. Cook over low heat, stirring constantly. Continue cooking until mixture completely coats a spoon when submerged. Remove from heat. Transfer to a large bowl. Add gelatin, mix well. Refrigerate until completely cool.

3. In mixer, whip cream until it has thickened to a "stiff" consistency. Transfer to another container. Reserve.

4. In clean mixer bowl, whip egg white until soft peaks form when whisk is removed. Should be light and fluffy.

5. Fold whipped cream into lemon mixture. Fold egg whites into lemon mixture. Do not overmix. Refrigerate until completely set, usually overnight.

(Yield: 10 to 12 servings)

Craisen (Dried Cranberry) Scone

3 1/3 cups unbleached flour
3/4 cup sugar
1 tablespoon baking powder
1/2 teaspoon salt
3/4 cup (1 1/2 sticks) butter, cool, cubed
3 large eggs
1 small orange, zested, juiced
Cream to make 1/4 cup plus 2 tablespoons when combined with
    above juice
2/3 cup craisens

1. Preheat oven to 350 degrees.

2. In a large bowl, sift together flour, sugar, baking powder and salt.
   Cut butter into flour mixture until it looks like coarse cornmeal.

3. In a medium bowl whisk egg (reserve 2 teaspoons egg and mix with
   2 teaspoons of water to make egg wash, set aside). To remaining egg
   add juice, cream, vanilla and zest and whisk until well blended.

4. Add egg mixture to flour mixture. Stir with a fork until dough cleans
   side of bowl. Stir in dried cranberries. Turn out onto a lightly floured
   smooth surface. Knead very lightly until well combined.

5. Pat into a disk 1 1/2-inches thick. Cut into 8 wedges. Space apart on
   an ungreased baking sheet. Brush scones with egg wash. Sprinkle
   with sugar if desired. Bake 20 to 25 minutes or until tester inserted
   comes out clean.

(Yield: 8 large scones)

Vanilla Cheesecake

Crumb Crust, unbaked
16 ounces (2 large packages) cream cheese, room temperature
1 cup sugar
3 large eggs, room temperature
1 1/2 teaspoons vanilla
1/4 teaspoon almond extract
3 cups sour cream, room temperature
Pinch of salt

Sour Cream Topping

3/4 cup sour cream
Flavoring of choice (examples: 1/4 teaspoon vanilla;
   1 to 2 tablespoons of liqueur (Amaretto, Frangelica, Kahlua)
3/4 cup whipping cream
1/4 cup powdered sugar (for chocolate topping, mix with
  2 tablespoons Ghirardelli cocoa powder)

1. Preheat oven to 350 degrees. Prepare crust.

2. In a large bowl with an electric mixer, beat together cream cheese and sugar until smooth. Add eggs, one at a time, blending well after each. Scrape down bowl occasionally. Add vanilla, almond extract, salt and sour cream. Beat well at medium speed.

3. Pour filling into prepared crust. Bake 50 minutes to 1 hour, until puffed and golden, with a firm jiggle when gently touched in the middle (cheesecake will be firm and settle when cooled). Cool on a wire rack. Cover and refrigerate overnight.

4. Prepare Topping: Blend sour cream and flavoring together. Reserve. Whip cream and sugar until firm peaks can form. Fold whipped cream and sour cream mixture together. Reserve.

5. Gently remove cheesecake from springform pan, lift and place on serving plate. Spread topping over top of cake.

(Yield: 1 9-inch cheesecake)

Crumb Crust for Cheesecake

2 cups cookie crumbs (graham crackers, gingersnaps or
   chocolate wafers whirled in processor to make crumbs)
1/2 cup nuts (walnuts, pecans, sliced almonds or hazelnuts;
   especially tasty when toasted)
1/4 teaspoon cinnamon
1/2 cup butter, room temperature

1. In processor with metal blade, combine crumbs, nuts and cinnamon.
   Add butter, blend well. Scrape bowl.

   Or,

   In a large bowl, combine crumbs, finely chopped nuts and cinnamon.
   Add butter and blend well using a pastry cutter, fork or fingers.

2. Line bottom of springform pan with parchment paper or grease.
   Paper should extend at least 1 inch from edges. Seat bottom into
   springform.

3. Press the mixture firmly and evenly into bottom and sides of pan.
   Pour in desired filling.

(Yield: 1 crumb crust)

Cheesecake Variations

Lemon

- 1 lemon, zested, juiced, combined with 1 tablespoon cornstarch. Add to sour cream.
- Graham cracker crust with toasted almonds.
- Add a couple drops almond extract to topping.

Blueberry Lemon

- Same as above with 1 small lemon.
- Fold in 1 to 1 1/2 cups blueberries before pouring into crust.

Pumpkin

- Reduce sour cream to 2 cups.
- Combine: 1 1/2 cups solid pack or cooked mashed pumpkin
              1 teaspoon cinnamon
              1/2 teaspoon ground ginger
              2 tablespoons molasses
              1/4 teaspoon ground cloves
              1/4 teaspoon freshly grated nutmeg
              1 tablespoon cornstarch
- Add pumpkin mixture with sour cream during assembly process.
- Gingersnap crust with toasted pecans.

Latté

- Whisk 1/2 to 3/4 cup cooled espresso with 1 to 1 1/2 teaspoons cornstarch. Add with the sour cream.
- Vanilla or chocolate wafer crust with sliced almonds or toasted hazelnuts.
- After topping is spread, sprinkle lightly with cinnamon or nutmeg.

Mocha

- Whisk 1/2 to 3/4 cup espresso with 1/2 cup Ghirardelli chocolate powder. Add with sour cream.
- Chocolate wafer crust with sliced almonds.
- Add a couple drops almond extract to topping. After spreading, lightly sift cocoa powder over or pipe on Ganache (recipe follows).

Chocolate Mint (Peppermint Patty)

- 1 tablespoon peppermint extract added with sour cream. Reduce vanilla to 1 teaspoon.
- Chocolate wafer crust with sliced almonds. No cinnamon.
- Instead of sour cream topping, spread with 1/2 recipe cooled Ganache (recipe follows).

Marionberry

- Reduce sour cream to 2 1/2 cups.
- Toss 1 1/2 cups frozen berries with 1/4 cup orange liqueur and 1 tablespoon cornstarch.
- Fold into filling before pouring into crust.
- Graham cracker crust with toasted hazelnuts.

Ganache

1 1/2 cups semi-sweet chocolate chips
2/3 cup cream

1. Prepare ganache by mixing together chocolate and cream. Microwave at medium (50%) power for 1 to 3 minutes, stirring each minute until chocolate begins to melt. Mixture may also be melted in top of double boiler or carefully over low heat on stovetop. With a small whisk, blend until smooth.

Savory Brioche Roll-ups

1 recipe cold Brioche dough
Egg wash (2 tablespoons beaten egg mixed with 2 tablespoons
  water)

Mushroom Filling

2 cups Monterey Jack cheese, shredded
1 cup Cheddar cheese, shredded
1 cup mushrooms, sautéed, cooled
1 tablespoon Parmesan cheese, grated
1/4 cup fresh parsley, chopped
1/4 cup green onion, chopped
1 tablespoon mayonnaise
Scant 1/4 teaspoon garlic powder
1/4 teaspoon fresh ground pepper
1 tablespoon mixed herbs (oregano, basil, thyme, tarragon)

Ham Filling

2 cups Cheddar cheese, shredded
1 cup Monterey Jack cheese, shredded
1 cup ham, chopped

Cheese Filling

1 tablespoon Parmesan cheese, grated
1/4 cup fresh parsley, chopped
1/4 cup green onion, chopped
1 tablespoon mayonnaise
Scant 1/4 teaspoon garlic powder
1/4 teaspoon fresh ground pepper
1 tablespoon mixed herbs

1. In large bowl, combine ingredients for filling of choice and
   mix well.

2. Punch down center of dough, pull sides of dough to center
   and lift from bowl. Shape and roll into rectangle 18-inches by
   8-inches by 1/2-inch thick. Work quickly as dough works best
   when cool.

3. Spread filling evenly over dough, leaving a 3/4-inch unfilled strip on long edges of dough. Press filling onto dough. Starting on a long side, snugly roll into a cylinder. Pinch to seal edge completely. Smooth.

4. With seam side down (should be 18-inches long), mark, then slice 1-inch thick rounds with a sharp knife. Place evenly on baking sheets lined with baking paper. Brush with egg wash. Cover lightly with plastic wrap and let rise in warm place until doubled in size, about 1 hour.

5. Meanwhile, preheat oven to 375 degrees. Bake 12 to 15 minutes, until golden brown. Cool briefly before removing from baking sheet.

(Yield: 18 pastries)

Mocha Chocolate Cake

1 cup Ghirardelli cocoa powder
1 cup warm water
1 cup strong coffee
2 3/4 cups unbleached flour
2 teaspoons baking soda
1/2 teaspoon baking powder
1/4 teaspoon salt
1 cup (2 sticks) butter, room temperature
2 cups sugar
4 large eggs

1. Preheat oven to 350 degrees. Grease two 9-inch round cake pans. Dust with flour or additional cocoa powder, tap out excess.

2. In a medium bowl, whisk together cocoa, water and coffee. Set aside. In another bowl, sift together the flour, baking soda, baking powder and salt. Set aside.

3. In a large bowl with electric mixer, beat together butter and sugar until light and fluffy. Add eggs one at a time, beating well after each. Scrape bowl occasionally throughout this process. Alternately add flour mixture (1/3 at a time) and cocoa mixture (1/2 at a time) to butter mixture, beating between additions. Pour batter into prepared pans.

4. Bake 45 minutes, until tester inserted into center of cake comes out clean.

5. Let cakes cool in pans for 15 minutes before turning out onto wire racks to finish cooling. Cool completely before frosting.

6. Frost layers with Espresso Buttercream Icing. Decorate with piped Ganache (see Cheesecake Variations), and espresso beans.

Espresso Buttercream Icing

2 cups (1 pound or 4 sticks) butter, room temperature
4 large egg yolks
1 teaspoon vanilla
1/4 cup espresso, cooled
5 cups powdered sugar, sifted

1. Cream butter until light and fluffy. Add yolks two at a time, beat
    well. Gradually add vanilla and espresso. Beat well, until completely
    integrated. Gradually add powdered sugar (1/2 at a time). Beat until
    smooth and fluffy. Scrape bowl occasionally throughout process.

2. Spread immediately and keep cake cool or refrigerated.

Cornmeal Rolls

1 1/2 tablespoons (1 1/2 packages) active dry yeast
3 tablespoons sugar
2 tablespoons powdered milk
1 1/4 cups warm water
3 1/2 cups unbleached flour
1/2 cup cornmeal
2 teaspoons salt
3 tablespoons butter, room temperature
Egg wash (2 tablespoons beaten egg with 2 tablespoons water)
1 tablespoon sesame or poppy seeds

1. Into a medium bowl, toss together yeast, sugar and dry milk. Add warm water. Stir briefly and gently. Let stand 5 minutes (should bubble).

2. In a large bowl, with a dough hook if electric mixer is used, mix together flour, cornmeal and salt. Add yeast mixture to flour mixture. Combine, then knead until the dough is elastic. Let rise in a warm place in a large covered bow until doubled, about 45 minutes to 1 hour. (A slightly warmed oven with a pan of just-boiled water on the bottom works well.)

3. Punch down the center of dough, pull sides of dough to center and lift from bowl. Knead, shape and press into an even disk shape. Cut into 8 even wedges. Shape each wedge into flattened disks, slightly thinner in the middle. Place on two ungreased baking sheets sprinkled with cornmeal. With a sharp knife, cut a full diameter shallow "X" into each roll. Brush with egg wash. Sprinkle with seed.

4. Let rise again until doubled, lightly covered with plastic wrap, about 30 minutes. Do not over-rise or rolls will collapse.

5. Meanwhile, preheat oven to 375 degrees. Bake 10 to 15 minutes.

(Yield: 8 rolls)

Cinnamon Knots

1 recipe cold Brioche dough
2 tablespoons butter, melted, cooled
2 teaspoons cinnamon
3/4 cup firmly packed brown sugar
3/4 cup walnuts, chopped
Egg wash (2 tablespoons beaten egg with 2 tablespoons water)

1. Punch down center of dough, pull sides of dough to center and lift from bowl onto a lightly floured surface. Shape and roll dough into a rectangle 16-inches by 10-inches by 1/2-inch thick. Press a crease with the side of hand lengthwise through middle of dough (dough will be folded here). Brush butter over entire surface of dough.
2. Sprinkle 1 1/2 teaspoons cinnamon over entire surface. Evenly distribute 1/2 cup brown sugar over half of surface to one side of crease (little dough should show through). Evenly distribute 1/2 cup nuts on sugared half of dough. Lightly press nuts into dough and sugar. Fold the uncovered side of dough onto the sugared side. Lightly roll. Work quickly as cool brioche dough is the most manageable and to preserve dough. If it gets too warm during process, gently lift onto a baking sheet, cover with plastic wrap and refrigerate.
3. Press a crease across center of dough in short direction. Sprinkle 1/2 teaspoon cinnamon over entire surface. Evenly distribute 1/4 cup brown sugar over half of dough to one side of crease. Evenly distribute nuts over same sugared half. Press nuts into sugared dough. Fold uncovered half of dough over sugared half. Lightly roll. Dough should be 12-inches long by 5-inches wide by 1 1/2-inches thick.
4. Mark 18 3/4-inch cuts in dough along long edge.
5. Slicing one strip at a time with a sharp knife, gently press and stretch strip into a 8-inch to 9-inch length. Tightly twist and form into a knot. Tuck top end in and bottom end under cinnamon knot. Place evenly on baking sheets lined with baking paper. Brush with egg wash. Cover lightly with plastic wrap and let rise in warm place until doubled, about 1 hour.
6. Meanwhile, preheat oven to 375 degrees. Bake 10 to 13 minutes, until lightly browned. Cool briefly and remove from sheet.

Desserts & Pastries

Notes

Lousiana Seafood Cakes with Cayenne Mayonnaise

2 pounds seafood (combination of cod, halibut, crab, shrimp, whatever)
2 cups celery, chopped
1 cup onion, chopped
1/2 cup green onions, chopped
4 cups dry bread crumbs
2 eggs, beaten
1 cup mayonnaise
1/4 cup Dijon mustard
1 teaspoons cayenne pepper
1 teaspoon Tabasco sauce
2 tablespoons lemon juice
2 tablespoons Worcestershire sauce
1/4 cup parsley, chopped
1 tablespoon salt
2 teaspoons pepper
1 cup buttermilk
1 cup cornmeal

Cayenne Mayonnaise

1 tablespoon Dijon mustard
1 cup mayonnaise
1/2 sour cream
2 teaspoons cayenne pepper

2 teaspoons paprika
1 lemon, juiced
Salt and pepper to taste

1. Coarsely chop seafood in processor. This may take several small batches. Place seafood into large mixing bowl.

2 Mix with all other crab cake ingredients (except buttermilk and cornmeal). This is best if mixed with your hands.

3. Form into 4-inch patties. Reserve.

2. Combine Cayenne Mayonnaise ingredients in bowl and refrigerate overnight. Stir again before serving.

3. Next day, dip patties in buttermilk and then in cornmeal. Fry in oil until browned lightly on both sides. Drain and keep warm in layers separated with paper towels. Serve with Cayenne Mayonnaise and a lemon wedge.

Main Dishes

Casserole a la Clohessy

2 to 3 yellow onions
3 garlic cloves, chopped
1 teaspoon salt
1 teaspoon pepper
1 pound ham, cooked, diced
4 cups French bread, cubed
1 head cauliflower, cut into florets, blanched
1/2 pound mushrooms, sliced
3/4 pound Cheddar cheese, grated
1/2 cup bread crumbs
1/2 cup Parmesan cheese, grated

White Sauce

1/2 cup (1 stick) butter
1 cup flour
1/2 teaspoon salt
Freshly grated nutmeg
3 to 4 cups milk

1. Preheat oven to 350 degrees.

2. In skillet, cook onions and garlic together with splash of oil for 3 to 5 minutes. Add mushrooms, sauté until tender. Add ham, salt and pepper and mix well.

3. In a lightly greased casserole dish, layer bread cubes with ham mixture and cauliflower. Reserve.

4. To make white sauce: Melt butter on low heat. Add flour. Mix well to form a paste.

5. Add 3 cups milk, salt and nutmeg. Continue cooking on low heat, stirring constantly.

6. When white sauce has thickened, remove from heat. Only add additional milk if sauce is too thick to pour.

7. Pour white sauce over bread and ham mixture in casserole dish. Top with Cheddar cheese.

8. In separate bowl, mix together bread crumbs and Parmesan cheese and sprinkle over casserole. Bake 30 to 40 minutes.

Whole Wheat Pasta a la Russe

1 pound whole wheat pasta (macaroni or other shape)
3 cups sour cream
4 cups cottage cheese
2 cups Cheddar, grated
2 red onions, sliced
4 green onions, chopped
3 green peppers, diced
4 cups (1 small head) cabbage, shredded
1 pound mushrooms, sliced
2 carrots, chopped
2 teaspoons caraway seeds
4 tablespoons soy sauce
1 tablespoon salt
Lots of pepper

1. Preheat oven to 350 degrees.

2. Combine sour cream, cheese, onions and green peppers.

3. Sauté cabbage, mushrooms, carrots and caraway seeds in 4 tablespoons of butter.

4. Boil the pasta and mix with some butter .

5. Combine everything. Add soy sauce and salt and pepper to taste. Place in buttered casserole dish; cover and bake 30 to 40 minutes or until completely cooked.

(Yield: 10 to 12 servings)

Ground Beef and Green Chile Pie

1 1/2 pounds ground beef
2 onions, chopped
2 red bell peppers, diced
2 green bell peppers, diced
1 tablespoon chili powder
1 tablespoon cumin
1/2 teaspoon cayenne
3 cups diced tomatoes, drained
1 cup green chilies, chopped
1 teaspoon salt
1 teaspoon pepper
1 cup corn
1 3/4 cups flour
2 tablespoons baking powder
1/2 teaspoon salt
1 1/2 cups milk
4 eggs
2 tablespoons butter, melted
2 ounces Monterey Jack cheese, grated
2 ounces Cheddar cheese, grated

1. Sauté ground beef, drain.

2. Add onions, peppers, chili powder, cumin, cayenne, tomatoes, chilies, salt and pepper.

3. Simmer 10 to 15 minutes.

4. Add corn.

5. Place in greased casserole dish. Refrigerate until ready to use. Bring out to room temperature.

6. Mix flour, baking powder and salt. Reserve.

7. Whisk together milk, eggs and melted butter.

8. Combine flour mixture and milk mixture to make batter. Pour over casserole.

9. Bake about 30 minutes. Should be golden brown and fully heated. Top with Cheddar and Jack cheeses. Bake 5 more minutes. Serve with salsa, sour cream.

(Yield: 10 to 12 servings)

Southwestern Chicken Hash

2 1/2 pounds red potatoes, cut in 1-inch cubes
1 large red bell pepper, chopped
1 cup fresh cilantro, coarsely chopped
2 cups chicken, cooked, diced
1 large onion, minced
1/4 cup fresh lime juice
3 large jalapeño peppers, seeded, minced
2 large garlic cloves, minced
3 tablespoons canned chicken broth
2 tablespoons Worcestershire sauce
1 tablespoon salt
2 teaspoons pepper
2 tablespoons vegetable oil
Salsa for topping

1. Cook potatoes in a large pot of boiling salted water until just tender. Drain and cool completely. Transfer to a mixing bowl

2. Sauté bell pepper, onion, jalapeños and garlic until tender. Add to potatoes. Add chicken, cilantro, lime juice, chicken stock, salt, pepper and Worcestershire sauce. Mix well.

3. Preheat broiler, pour oil into 12-inch diameter broiler-proof skillet. Add hash and pour into skillet. Broil until top browns (about 5 minutes).

4. Using spatula, turn browned portion over in sections. Broil until top is brown (about 5 minutes). Turn browned portion over again in sections.

5. Press into solid round and cook until crusty and brown (about 5 minutes). Slide hash out of skillet onto platter. Top with salsa.

(Yield: 10 to 12 servings)

Hint

This is great as a brunch dish, topped with eggs!

Main Dishes

Chicken Parmigiana

5 garlic cloves, chopped
3 onions, diced fine
1 yellow squash, sliced thin
1 zucchini, sliced thin
1 pound mushrooms, sliced
4 cups diced tomatoes, drained
1 1/2 cups artichoke hearts, drained, chopped
1 tablespoon thyme
1 tablespoon dried basil
1 tablespoon salt
Bay leaf
1 cup black olives (preferably Kalamata), chopped
4 cups chicken, cooked, cubed
1 cup green olives, chopped
1/2 cup bread crumbs
1/2 cup Parmesan cheese, grated
1 cup Mozzarella cheese, grated or sliced

1. Preheat oven to 350 degrees.

2. Sauté garlic, onion, zucchini and squash until tender.

3. Add mushrooms, tomatoes, artichoke hearts, thyme, basil, salt and bay leaf.

4. Add olives and chicken. Simmer 15 to 20 minutes.

5. Butter a large casserole dish.

6. Pour half of the mixture into dish, top with half of the cheeses and breadcrumbs. Repeat with remaining ingredients.

7. Bake about 30 minutes until golden brown.

(Yield: 12 servings)

Fall Vegetable Risotto

1/2 cup olive oil
10 garlic cloves
4 onions, chopped
6 carrots, sliced thin
1/2 bunch celery, chopped
2 red bell peppers
2 green bell peppers
2 yellow squash
1 cup sun-dried tomatoes
1/2 cup fresh basil
1 cup fresh parsley
2 cups Arborio rice
Vegetable stock (may need up to 10 cups)
1 to 2 cups white wine
2 cups Parmesan cheese

1. Finely mince garlic, onions, carrots, celery in food processor. Reserve.

2. Mince peppers and squash. Reserve.

3. Chop sun-dried tomatoes, basil and parsley. Reserve.

4. In thick bottom stock pot, heat olive oil, add onion and carrot mixture. Sauté for 5 minutes.

5. Add rice. Mix well to coat. Add generous amount of salt and pepper. Have lots of vegetable stock ready.

6. Add 2 to 3 cups of stock. Simmer risotto until most liquid is absorbed. Stir bottom well. Keep adding broth in 2 to 3 cup batches. Also add white wine. It may take up to 10 cups of liquid to "cook" risotto. Mixture will needs to cook at least 20 to 30 minutes. When tender, add Parmesan, reserved basil, parsley, salt and pepper, tomatoes and bell peppers.

7. Stir to combine. Adjust salt and pepper. Add peas at last minute before serving. Needs a lot of salt. Remove from heat. This will re-thicken. Adjust consistency with additional stock.

8. Garnish with Parmesan, parsley. Serve piping hot.

(Yield: 10 to 12 servings)

Eggplant Patties with Roasted Garlic Mayonnaise

3 eggplants, peeled
Vegetable stock
2 cups breadcrumbs
2 cups Parmesan cheese
1/2 cup green onions, chopped
1/4 cup fresh basil, chopped
1/4 cup fresh parsley, chopped
4 eggs
3 cloves garlic, chopped
1/4 cup white wine
1/4 cup lemon juice
1 tablespoon cumin
1 tablespoon paprika
1 tablespoon salt

Roasted Garlic Mayonnaise

4 to 6 bulbs garlic
2 cups mayonnaise
1 cup sour cream
1/2 cup green onion
1/2 cup parsley
2 tablespoons tomato paste
2 lemons, juiced
Salt and pepper

1. Prepare Roasted Garlic Mayonnaise: Cut the tops off of garlic. Place on tray in oven for 35 to 45 minutes (do not peel). Bake until very tender. Cool. When cool, press the garlic out (like a paste) and save.

2. Process together mayonnaise, sour cream, onion, parsley, garlic paste, tomato paste, lemon juice and salt and pepper to taste. Reserve.

3. Prepare eggplant: Cover eggplant with vegetable stock or water. Bring to a boil. Reduce heat. Simmer 8 to 10 minutes until very tender. Drain well.

2. Place eggplant in bowl. Mash well.

3. Add bread crumbs, Parmesan cheese, green onions, fresh basil and parsley, eggs, garlic, white wine, lemon juice, cumin, paprika and salt.

4. Mix well. Form into patties and coat with breadcrumbs, add more breadcrumbs if necessary. Bake 8 to 10 minutes or fry on griddle. Keep warm.

5. Serve 2 patties per person with Roasted Garlic Mayonnaise.

(Yield: 12 to 14 servings)

Hint

Keep extra patties in refrigerator. They make great sandwiches. Recipe can be halved.

Main Dishes

Bleu Cheese Meatloaf

2 1/2 pounds ground beef
1 green bell pepper, diced
1 red bell pepper, diced
2 yellow onions, chopped fine
8 garlic cloves, chopped
1 cup dry bread crumbs
2 eggs
4 tablespoons Dijon mustard
1 tablespoon salt
2 teaspoons pepper
2 tablespoons Worcestershire sauce
1 teaspoon Tabasco sauce

Cheese mixture

2 cups bleu cheese, crumbled
2 cups Monterey Jack cheese, grated
1/2 cup mayonnaise

1. In separate bowl, combine cheeses and mayonnaise. Mix well. Reserve.

2. Mix meatloaf ingredients in large bowl with hands until everything is well combined. Divide meat in half and spread each portion 3/4-inch thick in a rectangle on waxed paper or aluminum foil.

3. Divide cheese mixture in half. Spread one portion of cheese mixture over one portion of the meat, leaving a 2-inch edge along one long side. Using paper as an aid, roll up the meat jelly roll style with the seam on the bottom. Tuck edges in. Repeat with other half of meat and remaining cheese. Transfer to baking or roasting pan. Spread tomato sauce or ketchup over meat before baking if desired.

4. Bake in a 350 degree oven about 1 hour. The meat should reach an internal temperature of 160 degrees. When done, remove from oven. Let rest before serving. Transfer to cutting board. Slice in 2-inch thick slices and serve with grilled onions and horseradish.

Chicken Tostados

8-10 chopped garlic
4 yellow onions, chopped
4 red bell peppers, julienned
4 green bell peppers, julienned
1 cup green chilies, chopped
2 cups tomatoes, drained
2 cups salsa
3 tablespoons cumin
3 tablespoons chili powder
1 tablespoon oregano
1 tablespoon red pepper flakes
Salt and pepper
12 chicken breasts, cooked, diced
Corn tortillas
Canola oil
Lettuce

1. Sauté garlic, onions, peppers, chilies, tomatoes and salsa.

2. Add cumin, chili powder, oregano, red pepper flakes and salt and pepper to taste.

3. Add chicken and simmer for 5 minutes, adjust seasonings.

4. Fry corn tortillas in canola oil. Drain well (can do early).

5. To serve: Place tortilla shell on a bed of lettuce. Fill with chicken mixture, garnish with salsa, sour cream, grated Jack cheese, green onions, black bean puree or refried beans.

(Yield: 10 to 12 servings)

Main Dishes

Chicken Shortcake with Herb Biscuits

3 medium yellow onions, chopped
4 carrots, diced
2 cups celery, chopped
1 pound mushrooms, sliced
1 tablespoon thyme
1 tablespoon salt
1 tablespoon pepper
2 pounds potatoes, cooked, cooled, diced
2 heads broccoli, blanched, cooled
8 to 10 chicken breasts, cooked, chopped
2 cups Parmesan cheese
Salt and pepper
Herb Biscuits

White Sauce

1/2 pound margarine or butter
1 1/2 cups flour
1/2 gallon milk
Salt and pepper
Freshly grated nutmeg

1. To make white sauce: Melt butter in heavy saucepan and add flour. Cook, stirring constantly, until mixture bubbles (to cook flour). Add milk, whisking constantly until mixture boils and thickens. Season to taste. Reserve.

2. Sauté onions, carrots, celery, mushroom, thyme, salt and pepper. Reserve.

3. Combine white sauce, onion mixture, chicken, Parmesan cheese and season to taste.

4. To serve: Split 1 1/2 Herb Biscuits and place in gratin dish. Spoon sauce over top of biscuits. Garnish with chopped parsley.

(Yield: 10 to 12 servings)

Mexican Chicken Lasagna

4 yellow onions, diced
4 to 5 garlic cloves, minced
2 red bell peppers, diced
4 cups salsa
1 teaspoon pepper
4 tablespoons chili powder
2 tablespoons cumin
1 pound lasagna noodles, cooked
3 cups Cheddar cheese, grated
2 cups hominy or corn
4 cups chicken breasts, cooked, cut into bite-sized pieces
3 cups Monterey Jack cheese, grated

Cheese Sauce

2 cups cottage cheese
2 eggs
1/2 cup parsley
1 cup diced green chilies

1. Sauté onions and garlic.

2. Add bell peppers, salsa, pepper, chili powder and cumin and cook about 10 minutes. Cool slightly.

3. In separate bowl, combine cottage cheese, eggs, parsley and green chilies.

4. Butter a lasagna pan, approx. 3-inches by 8-inches by 12-inches.

5. Assemble in layers (noodles, cheese filling, hominy, chicken, sauce and cheese), repeating 2 more times.

6. Bake in a preheated 350 degree oven about 45 minutes. Let rest before serving.

(Yield: 12 to 14 servings)

Main Dishes

Cauliflower and Potato Curry with Coconut Milk and Lime Juice

1/2 cup olive oil
8 garlic cloves, chopped
2 onions, diced
2 tablespoons curry powder
1 tablespoon red pepper flakes
3 carrots, sliced
10 potatoes, sliced
1 head cauliflower, cut into florets, blanched
1 tablespoon salt
2 cups vegetable stock
1/2 cup prunes, chopped
1 cup peas
1 cup canned coconut milk
2 limes, juiced
1/2 bunch cilantro, chopped

1. Sauté garlic and onions in olive oil in large, deep skillet.

2. When tender, add curry powder and red pepper flakes.

3. Cook 2 to 3 minutes, add carrots and potatoes.

4. Mix well, sauté for 5 minutes and add cauliflower and salt.

5. Cook 3 to 5 minutes and add vegetable stock and prunes.

6. Bring to a boil, simmer for 10 minutes or until vegetables are tender.

7. Add peas, coconut milk, lime juice and cilantro.

8. Garnish with toasted coconut

(Yield: 10 to 12 servings)

Hominy, Tomato and Green Chile Casserole

1 1/2 cups yellow onion, chopped
2 garlic cloves, minced
2 tablespoons olive oil
15-ounce can white hominy, rinsed, drained
15-ounce can yellow hominy, rinsed, drained
2 cups tomatoes, peeled, seeded, chopped
4-ounce can hot green chilies or mild green chilies, chopped
3 tablespoons tomato paste
1 tablespoon ground cumin
1 tablespoon chili powder
1/2 teaspoon cayenne pepper
1 cup grated Monterey Jack cheese (about 3 ounces)
Jalapeños
Lemon juice
Lime juice

1. In a skillet, cook the onion and the garlic in the oil over moderately low heat, stirring until the onion is softened.

2. Stir in the hominies, tomatoes, chilies, tomato paste, spices, salt and pepper to taste, and simmer the mixture, stirring occasionally for 10 to 15 minutes.

3. Transfer the mixture to a greased 2 1/2-quart baking dish, sprinkle the Monterey Jack over it and bake the casserole in the middle of a pre-heated 350 degree oven for 30 minutes or until the cheese is golden.

(Yield: 4 as a main dish or 6 to 8 as a side dish)

Pollo Pepitoria

(Chicken Provençal)

This is the very first dish I prepared at Le Poulet Rouge and, coincidentally, one of my favorites.

3 tablespoons olive oil
8 chicken breast halves, skin removed
8 to 10 cloves garlic, peeled
1 1/2 cups almonds (whole, with skins)
6 slices French bread, cut into 1-inch slices
1 bay leaf
2 teaspoons salt
1 teaspoon pepper
2 cups chicken stock
1 cup mayonnaise
1 lemon, juiced

1. Brown chicken breasts in olive oil, approximately 2 minutes on each side. Remove and reserve.

2. Add garlic, almonds, bay leaf, bread to skillet. Cook approximately 3 minutes.

3. Take everything out of skillet and using processor, grind into a paste. Put back into skillet.

4. Add chicken stock, mayonnaise, lemon, salt and pepper on medium heat, slowly bring to a simmer.

5. Add browned chicken breasts and cook about 5 minutes. Make sure chicken is completely cooked. Add salt and pepper if necessary.

(Yield: 8 to 10 servings)

Hint

This is good served over rice or egg noodles.

Chicken and Cheese Casserole

2 1/2 cups chicken, cooked, cubed
2 1/2 cups milk
3/4 cup heavy cream
3 slices bacon, chopped
1 cup green onions, chopped
3 tablespoons butter
1 1/4 cups Brioche or French bread, cubed in 2-inch pieces
2 tablespoons flour
6 eggs
1 1/2 tablespoons parsley, chopped fine
1/4 teaspoon black pepper
Salt to taste
1 teaspoon Tabasco sauce
1 cup Mozzarella cheese, cubed
1/2 cup Parmesan cheese

1. Preheat oven to 350 degrees. Bring milk and cream just to a boil. Turn off heat.

2. Cook bacon over medium-high heat until crisp, reserving drippings. Crumble bacon and set aside.

3. In same skillet, sauté onions in bacon drippings until wilted.

4. Add butter, then bread cubes. Toss until cubes turn golden, set aside.

5. Whisk together flour and enggs until smooth.

6. Add chicken, parsley, salt, peppers and Tabasco.

7. Stir in warm milk.

8. Pour mix into well greased 13-inch by 9-inch by 2-inch casserole dish.

9. Sprinkle Mozzarella cheese over casserole, then add bread/onion mixture, which should sink slightly into casserole.

10. Sprinkle with Parmesan cheese and bacon.

11. Bake for 30 to 40 minutes, until casserole is set and lightly browned.

(Yield: 10 to 12 servings)

Main Dishes

Chicken with Apricots and Olives

8 chicken breasts, halved, skinless, boneless
1 cup Kalamata olives, drained, pitted
1 cup apricots, whole, dried
1 cup dry white wine
1/4 cup capers
1 orange, zested
1/2 cup orange juice
1/4 cup cider vinegar
3 tablespoons dried basil
2 tablespoons olive oil
6 cloves garlic, minced
1 cup firmly packed brown sugar
1 teaspoon salt
1 teaspoon pepper

1. Combine chicken, olives, apricots, wine, capers, orange zest, orange juice, vinegar, basil, oil, and garlic. Cover and refrigerate overnight.

2. Arrange chicken in baking pan in a single layer and pour marinade over chicken. Sprinkle sugar evenly over chicken.

3. Bake uncovered until chicken is fully cooked (approximately 15 minutes).

4. Serve with rice and additional sauce, garnished with a thin orange slice and parsley.

(Yield: 8 servings)

Salads

Chicken and Smoked Turkey Salad with Cranberry Hazelnut Dressing

4 cups cooked chicken, cubed in 1-inch pieces
4 cups smoked turkey, cubed in 1-inch pieces
1 cup Provolone cheese, 1-inch pieces
1 1/2 cups celery, chopped
1 cup green onions, chopped
1/2 cup parsley, chopped
3/4 cup hazelnuts, toasted, chopped
2 cups grapes
2 lemons, juiced
Salt and pepper

Dressing

1 tablespoon dry tarragon
1 cup hazelnuts, toasted, chopped
1 cup dried cranberries
1/2 cup raspberry vinegar
1 1/2 cups sour cream
1 1/2 cups mayonnaise
1/4 cup Dijon mustard
Salt and pepper

1. Mix salad ingredients well. Reserve.

2. In processor combine all dressing ingredients and blend well. If mixing by hand, chop hazelnuts and dried cranberries and fold into other ingredients.

3. Fold dressing into salad ingredients. Adjust salt and pepper to taste.

Hint

To toast hazelnuts: Place nuts on a baking sheet and toast in a preheated 350 degree oven for 8 to 10 minutes. Be sure to give the nuts a shake partway through toasting to brown evenly. Remove from oven. Cool slightly. Using palms of hands, rub off as much of the loose skin from the nuts as possible and discard skin. Never chop nuts until cool.

Dixie-Style Potato Salad

20 large red potatoes, cooked, cut into quarters
1 cup green onions, chopped
2 red peppers, diced
1 green pepper, diced
4 hard-cooked eggs, chopped
3/4 cup green olives, chopped
3/4 cup black olives, chopped
3/4 cup sweet relish
1 1/2 cups celery, chopped
Salt and pepper
Pinch of cayenne

Dressing

1 1/2 cups mayonnaise
1 1/2 cups sour cream
1/4 cup Dijon mustard
1/3 cup red wine vinegar
Salt and pepper

1. Mix together salad ingredients in large bowl. Set aside.

2. Process dressing ingredients until thoroughly combined.

3. Pour over salad, stir together.

Chicken and Smoked Ham Salad

6 cups chicken breasts, cut in 1-inch pieces
2 cups ham, diced
10 red potatoes, cut in half, sliced, cooked
3 carrots, blanched, cut in half, sliced thin
2 zucchini, split lengthwise, sliced thin
1 cup celery, diced
1 cup green onions, chopped
1/2 cup parsley, chopped
Salt and pepper

Dressing

2 cups mayonnaise
2 cups sour cream
1/2 cup Dijon mustard
1 cup red wine vinegar
3 tablespoons dried basil
2 teaspoons salt
1 teaspoon pepper

1. Cook potatoes until almost done, add carrots and continue to cook until vegetables are tender. Drain, rinse under cold water to stop cooking.

2. Combine all salad ingredients and mix well.

3. Combine dressing ingredients and add to salad ingredients, mix well and adjust seasonings.

Cobb Salad

8 cups chicken breasts, cooked and chopped
10 strips bacon, cooked crisp, chopped
1/2 pound button mushrooms, cleaned, halved
6 Roma tomatoes, cut in wedges
1 cup black olives, chopped
1/2 bunch parsley, chopped
2 cups celery, chopped
1 8-ounce bag pasta, cooked (optional)
1 cup green onions, chopped
3 avocados, diced
1 cup bleu cheese, crumbled

Basil Vinaigrette

2/3 cup red wine vinegar
1 cup olive oil
1 cup canola oil
4 garlic cloves, chopped
1 1/2 tablespoons Dijon mustard
2 tablespoons dried basil
2 teaspoons salt
1 teaspoon pepper

1. Put vinaigrette ingredients in a jar and shake to combine.

2. Toss everything except avocados with Basil Vinaigrette. Add avocados and gently fold into salad. Top with bleu cheese.

Broccoli-Sesame Salad

3 heads broccoli, chopped, blanched
2 carrots, peeled, thinly sliced, blanched
1 yellow squash, cut in 1-inch strips
1/2 cup green onions, chopped
1/2 pound (5 cups) button mushrooms, sliced

Dressing

1 1/2 cups olive oil
2 tablespoons sesame seeds
4 garlic cloves, minced
1 1/2 teaspoons Dijon mustard
1/4 cup red wine vinegar
Salt and pepper to taste
Rice wine vinegar

1. Heat oil in saucepan and add sesame seeds. Heat over medium heat until seeds just barely start to brown. Remove from heat and let stand for 5 minutes.

2. Add garlic to still-hot oil. It should sizzle but not brown. Cool.

3. Put oil mixture in processor* with remaining ingredients and process until throughly combined. Adjust salt and pepper.

4. Combine vegetables in salad bowl, add dressing.

5. When mixing salad, adjust salt and pepper, add a splash of rice wine vinegar.

*If a creamier dressing is desired, an egg may be added to the vinegar, mustard and oil mixture while the machine is running.

Broccoli Walnut Salad

3 heads broccoli, cut into florets, blanched
1 cup green onions, chopped
1 1/2 cups green olives, chopped
2 cups walnuts, toasted, chopped

Dressing

1 cup sour cream
1 1/2 cups mayonnaise
Salt and pepper
2 tablespoons Dijon mustard
2 lemons, juiced
Salt and pepper

1. Mix dressing ingredients together in food processor. Reserve.

2. Combine vegetables and walnuts in bowl.

3. Toss with dressing. Adjust salt and pepper to taste.

Tortellini Chicken Salad

1 pound tortellini, cooked al dente (or 1 pound dry pasta, rotelle, shells)
4 cups cooked chicken breasts, cut in julienned strips
2 zucchini, julienned
4 carrots, julienned
2 cups celery, julienned
1 cup green onions, chopped
1 red bell pepper, julienned
1 green bell pepper, julienned
6 Roma tomatoes, cut in strips

Dressing

4 garlic cloves, chopped
2 tablespoons Dijon mustard
2 teaspoons salt
1 teaspoon black pepper
1/4 cup fresh basil, chopped
2 lemons, juiced
3/4 cup red wine vinegar
2 1/2 to 3 cups olive oil

1. Combine all dressing ingredients and mix well.

2. Combine all salad ingredients and toss to mix. Pour dressing over salad and mix well.

Apricot Ginger Chicken Salad

2 cups celery, chopped
2 carrots, blanched, cut in half, sliced
1 head broccoli, cut in florets, blanched
2 red bell peppers, julienned
1 cup almonds, chopped coarsely
1 cup apricots, roughly chopped
8 cups chicken breasts, cooked, cut into small pieces
   (approximately 6 whole breasts)
4 to 5 oranges, seeded, cut in sections
Salt and pepper

Dressing

1 1/2 cups mayonnaise
1 1/2 cups sour cream
8 ounces cream cheese, softened
3 oranges, zested, juiced
1 1/2 teaspoons salt
1 1/2 teaspoons pepper
1 1/2 teaspoons curry powder
1 tablespoon ground ginger
2 tablespoons fresh ginger, peeled, grated
1 lemon, juiced
1 cup coconut, shredded
2 tablespoons crystallized ginger

1. Mix together vegetables and chicken, set aside.

2. In processor, combine dressing ingredients. Blend well.

3. Pour dressing over salad, toss well.

Hint

This makes a large batch of dressing. Keep on hand for other uses.
This works well as a dip for fresh vegetables.

Tex-Mex Potato Salad

30 large potatoes, sliced 1/4-inch thick
1 cup olive oil
1 cup green onions, chopped
1 bunch cilantro, chopped
4 garlic cloves, minced
2 cups Cheddar cheese, grated
2 teaspoons chili powder
1 teaspoon cayenne pepper
1 teaspoon black pepper
1 teaspoon white pepper
1 tablespoon ground coriander
2 tablespoons paprika
1 tablespoon cumin
1 tablespoon salt

1. Cook potatoes until just tender. Drain, but keep warm.

2. Combine spices in a bowl. Heat oil and add spice mixture and cook
   for 15 seconds, stirring constantly.

3. Add oil mixture to potatoes and toss, add salt, green onion, cilantro
   and cheese. Combine well. Add salt to taste. Serve at room
   temperature or slightly warm.

Smoked Turkey and Chicken Salad with Tarragon and Walnuts

4 cups smoked turkey, cut in 1-inch cubes
4 cups cooked chicken breasts, cut in 1-inch cubes
1 pound (approx. 2 cups) Swiss cheese, julienned
1 1/2 cups celery, chopped
2 cups seedless grapes, red and green mixed, whole
1 cup walnuts, toasted, chopped
1 cup green onions, chopped
1/2 cup parsley, chopped
Salt and pepper
1 lemon, juiced

Dressing

2 garlic cloves, chopped
2 eggs
1/3 cup Dijon mustard
2 tablespoons dried tarragon
2 teaspoons salt
1 teaspoon pepper
1 cup red wine vinegar
1 1/2 cups olive oil
1 1/2 cups canola oil } Mixed together

1. Mix salad ingredients well. Reserve.

2. In processor, combine garlic, eggs, mustard, tarragon, salt and pepper. Process about 2 minutes.

3. Add oils slowly to make a thick, creamy dressing.

4. Add dressing to salad ingredients, adjust salt and pepper to taste.

Chicken Couscous Salad

Couscous

Bring 2 cups water to the boil. Add 1 cup couscous; stir; remove from heat; let sit for 10 minutes; "fluff" into colander ; cool, drain well; toss with oil.

Salad

8-10 oranges, cut into sections
Prepared couscous
6 cups cooked chicken, cut in 1-inch pieces
2 cups green onions, choped
3 red bell peppers, julienned
3 green bell peppers, julienned
1 bunch celery, chopped
1 1/2 cup currants
1 fresh pineapple, diced
1 cup pine nuts
Parsley
Salt and pepper
2 lemons, juiced

Dressing

4 oranges, zested
2 cups orange juice
1 cup white vinegar
2 cups olive oil
1 cup canola oil
1 tablespoon allspice
1 tablespoon cinnamon
1 tablespoon salt
1 tablespoon coriander

1. Prepare couscous. Be sure to cool before adding to salad.

2. Mix salad ingredients; mix dressing ingredients.

3. Add only enough dressing to salad to coat ingredients.

Kate and Karen's Corn Bread Salad

1 batch corn bread, recipe below
1 red bell pepper, diced
1 green bell pepper, diced
1 red onion, diced
1/2 cup parsley, chopped
1 bunch cilantro, chopped
2 cups green onion, chopped
4 garlic cloves, chopped
2 to 3 jalapeño peppers, chopped
Salt and pepper
1 cup olive oil
1/4 cup white vinegar
1/2 cup lime juice (approximately 4 limes)

1. Cut corn bread into even chunks. Toast for 1 hour at
   200 degrees until crispy. Cool.

2. In bowl, combine corn bread, peppers, onions, parsley, cilantro,
   onion, garlic and jalapeño peppers. Toss well.

3. Combine olive oil, vinegar and lime juice. Pour over corn bread
   mixture and toss well.

Corn Bread

3 1/2 cups flour
1 1/2 cups cornmeal
1 cup sugar
3 tablespoons baking powder
2 teaspoons salt
2 3/4 cups milk
2/3 cup butter, melted
2 eggs, lightly beaten

1. Combine flour, cornmeal, sugar, baking powder and salt. Reserve.

2. Combine milk, butter and eggs. Combine with dry ingredients.

3. Mix well; pour into greased, 9-inch by 13-inch pan. Bake in
   preheated 350 degree oven for 45 to 50 minutes.

Minestrone Salad with Basil Garlic Mayonnaise Dressing

8 ounces shell pasta or rotelle, cooked
1 cup garbanzo beans, rinsed, drained
2 cups celery, sliced
3 to 4 zucchini, cut in 1/2-inch slices
8 large potatoes, quartered, cooked, cooled
1/2 cup parsley, chopped
1 red onion, diced
2 red bell peppers, diced or juilienned
2 green bell peppers, diced or juilienned
Salt and pepper
Parmesan cheese
Roma tomatoes, sliced for garnish

Basil-Garlic Dressing

2 cups mayonnaise
1 cup sour cream
1 cup Parmesan cheese
2 tablespoons fresh basil, chopped
4 to 5 garlic cloves, chopped
1/2 cup red wine vinegar
Salt and pepper

1. Combine salad ingredients and mix well. Salt and pepper to taste. Reserve.

2. Combine dressing ingredients. Combine with salad mixture.

3. Garnish with additional Parmesan cheese and sliced Roma tomatoes.

Leek and Potato Salad or Vichyssoise Potato Salad

20 red potatoes, quartered
3 large leeks, cut into rings, washed well
4 garlic cloves, chopped
4 red bell peppers, diced
Olive oil for sautéeing
Salt
Pepper
1/2 cup parsley, chopped
2 tablespoons Dijon mustard

Dressing

1/2 cup cider vinegar
4 tablespoons green peppercorns
2 tablespoons Dijon mustard
1 1/2 cups mayonnaise
1 1/2 cups yogurt or sour cream
Salt and pepper to taste

1. Cook potatoes. Drain, cool, reserve.

2. Sauté leeks in oil until soft, about 10 minutes.

3. Add garlic and bell peppers. Sauté for 5 minutes or until tender. Cool and reserve.

4. Combine potatoes, salt, pepper, parsley and mustard. Mix well with leek mixture.

5. Process dressing ingredients. Add to potato mixture and combine well.

Potato Salad with Green Beans and Watercress

16 large potatoes, quartered, cooked, drained, cooled
1 1/2 pounds green beans, blanched, cut in 1-inch pieces
2 bunches watercress, stem removed
5 radishes, sliced thin
1 red onion, sliced, roughly chopped
1 cup green onions, chopped
1/4 cup parsley, chopped
2 tablespoons Dijon mustard
2 tablespoons red wine vinegar to toss with salad
Salt
Pepper

Dressing

8 garlic cloves, chopped
3 tablespoons green peppercorns
1/2 cup Dijon mustard
1 1/2 cups sour cream
1 1/2 cups mayonnaise
1/4 cup cider vinegar
Salt and pepper
2 lemons, juiced

1. Combine salad ingredients well, reserve.

2. Combine garlic and peppercorns in processer and chop well.

3. Add mustard, sour cream, mayonnaise, vinegar, salt, pepper and lemon juice. Process.

4. Add dressing to salad ingredients and mix well. Adjust salt and pepper.

Oriental Chicken Salad

2 lemons, juiced
4 to 5 carrots, grated
8 cups chicken breasts, cooked, chopped
1/2 pound bean sprouts
1 head Napa cabbage or bok choy, julienned
1 cup water chestnuts, chopped or sliced
1/2 small head red cabbage, cut fine
1 cup green onions, chopped
1 cup almonds, chopped
Salt and pepper

Dressing

4 garlic cloves, chopped
2 tablespoons fresh ginger, chopped or grated fine
2 eggs
1/4 cup Dijon mustard
1/2 cup white wine vinegar
1/2 cup rice wine vinegar
2 lemons, juiced
3 tablespoons soy sauce
2 tablespoons sugar
2 teaspoons salt
1 teaspoon pepper
2 1/2 cups canola oil
1/2 cup sesame oil
1/2 cup olive oil

1. For dressing: Process garlic and ginger.

2. Add eggs, mustard, vinegars, lemon juice, soy sauce, sugar, salt and pepper.

3. Combine oils and slowly add to ginger mixture with processor running. Reserve.

4. Combine salad ingredients and toss with dressing.

Pauline's Chicken Salad

Salad

8 cups chicken breasts, cooked, cut in 1-inch cubes
1 cup red grapes
1 cup green grapes
3 Granny Smith apples, cut into 1-inch slices
1 cup celery, chopped
1 1/2 cups walnuts
1 cup green onions
1/2 cup parsley, chopped
1 to 2 lemons, juiced

Dressing

4 egg yolks
2 tablespoons Dijon mustard
1 tablespoon salt
1 tablespoon pepper
4 tablespoons horseradish
2 tablespoons juniper berries
1 cup white vinegar
3 1/2 cups canola oil

1. Combine salad ingredients and toss well to coat all with lemon juice.
   Reserve.

2. Combine dressing ingredients and process well.

3. With processor running, slowly add canola to dressing in thin stream.
   If dressing is too thick, thin with cream. Adjust salt and pepper to
   taste.

4. Pour dressing over salad ingredients and mix well.

Hint

If you can't find juniper berries, toss a little gin into the dressing. Gin is
flavored with juniper berries.

Red Bean and Rice Salad

Beans

4 cups kidney beans
2 tablespoons thyme
2 tablespoons basil
2 tablespoons oregano
2 tablespoons cumin
2 tablespoons salt
1 tablespoon cinnamon
1 tablespoon corriander
1 teaspoon cayenne
1 teaspoon paprika

Rice

1 cup rice
2 cups water
2 tablespoons butter
1 tablespoon salt

Salad

Prepared rice
Prepared beans
4 garlic cloves, chopped
1 bunch celery, diced small
3 red bell peppers, diced
3 green bell peppers, diced
2 cups green onions, chopped
1 cup parsley, chopped

Dressing

3 cups salsa
1 cup red vinegar
1 to 2 jalapeño peppers, seeded, chopped
2 lemons, juiced
3 limes, juiced
1 tablespoon salt
1 teaspoon pepper

1. The day before: Cook kidney beans. Bring to a boil, let sit for
   1 hour. Reheat and add seasonings. Cook 1 hour or until tender.
   Drain, cool. Reserve

2. Bring water and salt to a boil and add rice and butter. Cook covered
   12 to 15 minutes until liquid is absorbed; drain, cool.

3. Combine dressing ingredients. Reserve.

4. Mix salad ingredients well with lots of salt and pepper, add dressing
   mixture.

Hint

When handling fresh jalapeños, it is a good idea to wear rubber gloves.
Wash all surfaces, including hands, after handling jalapeños and be
careful not to rub your eyes.

Saffron Rice Salad

Rice, cooked (recipe follows)
1 cup currants
1 cup walnuts, chopped
2 red bell peppers, diced
1 green bell pepper, diced
1 cup green onions
1/2 cup parsley, chopped
1/4 cup mint, chopped
2 Granny Smith apples, grated
1 1/2 cups celery, finely diced
Salt, pepper, lemon juice

Dressing

4 garlic cloves, chopped
2 oranges, zested, juiced
2 teaspoons cinnamon
2 teaspoons coriander
2 teaspoons ginger
1 1/2 teaspoons salt
1/4 cup lemon juice (about 3 lemons)
1/4 cup white vinegar
1/2 cup rice wine vinegar
1 1/2 cups canola
1 1/2 cups olive oil

Rice

6 cups water
3 tablespoons butter, melted
1 teaspoon saffron threads, soaked in 3 tablespoons of water
1 bay leaf
1 tablespoon salt
2 teaspoons turmeric
3 cups dry rice

1. The day before: Bring water to a boil. Add butter, saffron, bay leaves, salt, turmeric, garam masala and rice. Cover and cook until all water is evaporated and small "dimples" appear. Remove from heat. Keep covered 15 to 20 minutes. Drain and cool. Reserve

2. Combine salad ingredients, toss well.

3. Combine dressing ingredients, add to salad ingredients, mix well.

Notes

Thai Chicken Salad

1 box angel hair pasta, quartered, cooked
6 cups chicken breasts, julienned
1 pound bean sprouts
2 green bell peppers, julienned
2 red bell peppers, julienned
2 to 3 cucumbers, thinly sliced

Dressing

2 limes, juiced
1/2 cup brown sugar
4 jalapeño peppers or 2 unseeded peppers
1 whole nutmeg, grated (about 1 teaspoon ground nutmeg)
2-inch piece fresh ginger, minced
1 cup fresh mint leaves
1/4 cup minced fresh basil
2 tablespoons fish sauce
2 1/2 cups canola oil
2 1/2 cups olive oil

1. Combine dressing ingredients except oils in food processor. Add oil in a thin stream to make a dressing.

2. Toss dressing with chicken and vegetables. Serve over lettuce and garnish with toasted almonds

Hint

Fish sauce, also known as 'nam pla' or 'nuoc nam' can be found in the oriental section of most large supermarkets or in an oriental food store.

Jalapeño-Tomato Pasta Salad

1 pound rotelle pasta, cooked
1 tablespoon olive oil
2 cups cherry tomatoes, halved or 12 Roma tomatoes, cut into chunks
1 red bell pepper, diced
1 green bell pepper, diced
1/2 cup green onions, sliced thin
1/4 cup cilantro, chopped
Salt and pepper

Dressing

8 cloves garlic, minced
1 red onion, roughly chopped
2 to 3 jalapeños, minced
1 cup red wine vinegar
1 cup salsa
2 cups olive oil
2 teaspoons salt
1 teaspoon pepper

1. For dressing: Mince garlic, onion and jalapeños in processor.

2. Add vinegar, oil, salsa, salt and pepper and mix.

3. Process until all ingredients are well blended. Reserve.

4. Cook pasta, drain, rinse and cool. Toss with olive oil to prevent pasta from sticking together.

5. Cut cherry tomatoes in half, mix with all other ingredients.

6. Toss with dressing, add salt and pepper to taste.

Rice, Asparagus and Cucumber Salad

Cooked rice, recipe follows
2 pounds asparagus, blanched, cut in 1-inch pieces
4 cucumbers, peeled, seeded, sliced 1/2-inch thick
2 red bell peppers, diced
2 cups green onion, chopped
Parsley
Salt and pepper
2 lemons, juiced

Dressing

1/4 cup Dijon mustard
1 cup white wine vinegar
1 cup lemon juice
5 tablespoons sugar
1 tablespoon dry powdered mustard
1 tablespoon salt
2 cups olive oil
2 cups canola oil
1/2 cup fresh dill, chopped
Salt and pepper

Rice

5 cups water
2 1/2 cups rice
1 1/2 teaspoons salt
2 tablespoons butter

1. To cook rice: Bring water and salt to a boil. Add rice and butter and simmer 15 to 20 minutes (covered) until liquid is absorbed. Let set off heat for 10 minutes. Rinse in cold water, drain, cool.

2. Combine all salad ingredients and mix well. Reserve.

3. Combine all dressing ingredients, mix well.

4. Combine dressing with salad ingredients and mix well. Salt and pepper to taste.

Four Bean Salad

Salad

3 cups black beans, rinsed, drained
3 cups red kidney beans, rinsed, drained
2 pounds green beans, blanched
1/2 can garbanzo beans, rinsed, drained
1/2 bunch celery, sliced thin
4 carrots, grated
1 red onion, diced
1/2 cup parsley, chopped
1/2 cup fresh dill, chopped
Salt and pepper
1/4 cup red wine vinegar

Dressing

6 to 8 garlic cloves, chopped
1 cup lemon juice
1 tablespoon oregano
1 tablespoon basil
1 tablespoon salt
1 tablespoon pepper
1/4 cup Balsamic vinegar
2 cups olive oil
2 cups canola oil

1. Combine salad ingredients in large bowl. Toss to mix.

2. Combine dressing ingredients in separate bowl. Mix well and pour over salad ingredients.

Fettuccine Salad
with Sun-Dried Tomato Dressing

1 pound fettuccine, broken into pieces
1 red bell pepper, diced
1 green bell pepper, diced
2 to 3 ounces salami or pepperoni, julienned
2 to 3 ounces provolone, julienned
1 cup black olives, chopped
1/2 cup parsley, chopped
1 cup green onions, chopped
1 cup Parmesan cheese
Salt and pepper

Sun-Dried Tomato Vinaigrette

1 cup chopped tomatoes
1/2 cup chopped fresh basil
1 cup red wine vinegar
2 cups olive oil
1 cup canola oil
Salt and pepper

1. Cook pasta. Rinse, drain, cool.

2. Add remaining salad ingredients, mix well. Set aside.

3. Combine vinaigrette ingredients.

3. Toss salad ingredients with vinaigrette. Mix well, season to taste.

Green Bean, Barley and Tomato Salad

4 cups water
1 tablespoon salt
2 cups barley
1 pound green beans, blanched, cut in 1-inch pieces
2 yellow squash, sliced thin
2 cups cherry tomatoes or 5 Roma tomatoes, quartered
1 cup green onions, chopped
1/2 cup parsley, chopped
1/2 cup pine nuts or walnuts, toasted if desired
Salt and pepper

Dressing

8 to 10 garlic cloves, chopped
1 cup lemon juice
1/4 cup white vinegar
1 tablespoon dried basil
1 tablespoon dried thyme
3 tablespoons Dijon mustard
Salt and pepper
2 cups olive oil
1 cup canola oil

1. Bring water to a boil and add salt and barley. Cover, reduce to a low simmer for 15 minutes or until all liquid is absorbed. Remove from heat, let stand covered for 15 to 20 minutes. Drain and cool. Toss barley in bowl (break-up lumps).

2. Add green beans, squash, tomatoes, onions, parsley, pine nuts and salt and pepper to taste. Mix well.

3. Combine dressing ingredients in separate bowl and mix well.

4. Pour over salad ingredients and toss to combine. Adjust seasonings to taste.

Barley-Broccoli Salad

2 yellow squash, cut into 1/2-inch slices
2 heads broccoli, blanch, drain, cool
4 carrots, grated
4 cups water
1 tablespoon salt
2 cups barley
6 Roma tomatoes, quartered
1 cup green onions, diced
1/2 cup parsley, chopped

Lemon-Basil Vinaigrette

8 garlic cloves, chopped
1 cup lemon juice (about 5 lemons)
1/4 cup white vinegar
1 cup green onions
1/2 cup fresh basil, chopped
2 tablespoons Dijon mustard
1 1/2 teaspoons salt
1 tablespoon dried basil
2 cups olive oil
1 cup canola oil

1. Blanch squash, broccoli and carrots. Chill.

2. Bring water to a boil. Add salt and barley. Cover, reduce to low simmer for 15 minutes or until all of the liquid is absorbed. Remove from heat, let stand covered 15 to 20 minutes. Cool. Pour into a bowl, chill.

3. Add blanched vegetables and tomatoes, green onion and parsley to barley. Mix.

4. Combine vinaigrette ingredients. Mix well.

5. Toss barley mixture with Lemon-Basil Vinaigrette. Adjust seasonings to taste.

Bistro Pasta Salad

1 pound pasta, cooked, cooled (rotelle, shells or mosticolli)
4 cups fresh spinach, chopped
2 cups cherry tomatoes, cut in half
3 cups artichoke hearts, chopped
1 1/2 cups black olives, chopped or sliced
1/2 cup green onions, chopped
1/2 cup red onion, chopped
1/2 cup fresh basil, chopped
1 cup Parmesan cheese, grated
Salt and pepper

Dressing

10 garlic cloves, chopped
2 cups sun-dried tomatoes, chopped
6 tablespoons tomato paste
1/2 cup basil leaves, chopped
1/2 cup Balsamic vinegar
1/2 cup red wine vinegar
1 cup tomato juice
1 1/2 cups canola oil
1 1/2 cups olive oil
2 teaspoons salt
1 teaspoon pepper

1. Combine salad ingredients in large bowl.

2. Combine dressing ingredients in separate bowl and mix well.

3. Pour dressing over salad ingredients and toss to combine.

Chicken Salad with Dill

For Salad

8 cups chicken, cooked, cubed
1 red pepper, julienned
1 green pepper, julienned
1 1/2 cups celery, chopped
1 to 2 baskets cherry tomatoes, cut in half
1 cup green onions, chopped
1/2 red onion, diced
1 tablespoon Dijon mustard
1/2 cup parsley, chopped fine
1/2 cup fresh dill, chopped
Salt and pepper

Dressing

2 to 3 garlic cloves
1 egg yolk
1 tablespoon sugar
1 tablespoon Dijon mustard
1/4 cup capers, rinsed, drained
2 tablespoons dill, chopped
1/2 cup red wine vinegar
2 cups canola oil
2 lemons, juiced

1. Combine salad ingredients in large bowl.

2. In processor, mince garlic. Add remaining ingredients except lemon juice, mix well.

3. Toss salad ingredients with dressing and lemon juice. Season with salt and pepper to taste. Serve on bed of lettuce.

Panzanella

2 loaves of French bread, cut into 2-inch pieces, toasted until light
  brown and crisp
4 cloves garlic, peeled and minced
1/2 small red onion, peeled and diced
1/2 cup Kalamata olives, pitted and chopped
1/2 cup packed fresh basil leaves, chopped
5 Roma tomatoes, trimmed, cut in eighths
1/3 cup red wine vinegar or Balsamic vinegar
3/4 cup olive oil
Salt and lots of ground pepper

1. Combine bread and vegetables.

2. Combine dressing ingredients and toss with salad. Let stand at room
    temperature for at least 1 hour before serving.

Hint

This recipe is best if good quality bread is used. We use French baguettes.

Spinach and Rotelle Salad

1 pound rotelle pasta
1/2 cup olive oil
6 anchovies, diced
3 cloves garlic, minced
1/2 cup pine nuts (walnuts may be substituted)
1 pound fresh spinach, cleaned and stemmed, cut in
   lengthwise strips
1/2 cup parsley, chopped
Salt and pepper to taste
Parmesan cheese

1. Cook pasta and toss with a splash of oil. Do not refrigerate!

2. Sauté anchovies, garlic and pine nuts until they are browned.

3. Add spinach to wilt.

4. Toss contents of pan with pasta in pasta dish.

5. Add parsley, salt and pepper.

6. Sprinkle with Parmesan cheese. Serve slightly warm.

Hint

This salad is best served immediately after preparation as spinach will discolor.

Chinese Vegetables

2 heads broccoli, cut into florets, blanched
6 carrots, sliced thin, blanched
1 pound snow peas, strings removed, blanched
1/2 pound bean sprouts
1 1/2 cups celery, julienned
2 red peppers, julienned
2 green peppers, julienned
1/2 large red cabbage, cut into long, thin strips
1 bunch green onions, cut at diagonal 1/2-inch long
1 bunch cilantro, chopped (optional)
2 tablespoons sesame seeds, toasted

For dressing

2 cloves garlic, minced
2 tablespoons fresh ginger, minced
1/4 cup sesame oil
3 cups canola oil
1 cup cider vinegar
1 cup soy sauce
2 teaspoons red pepper flakes
2 tablespoons sugar
2 lemons, juiced

1. Combine all salad vegetables together in large bowl, set aside.

2. In food processor, mince garlic and ginger.

3. With processor running, add remaining dressing ingredients, mix well.

4. Pour over vegetables, toss well. Refrigerate unused dressing.

5. Process all ingredients except sesame seeds.

6. Add sesame seeds.

Notes

Notes

Notes

Broccoli Coleslaw

3 heads broccoli, florets whole, stems grated. Do not blanch!
1 red onion, diced
1 cup raisins
2/3 cup sunflower seeds, toasted and salted
Salt
Pepper

Dressing

1 1/2 cups mayonnaise
1 1/2 cups sour cream
1/2 cup cider vinegar, to thin
1 teaspoon sugar
2 teaspoons salt
1 teaspoon pepper

1. Mix dressing ingredients together. Reserve.

2. Place grated broccoli stems and florets in a bowl. A processor fitted with a grating disk is best, although you can grate by hand.

3. Add other salad ingredients. Mix with dressing.

Notes

Italian Pasta Salad

1 pound bag rotelle pasta
1 pound green beans, cut in 1-inch pieces
2 small zucchini, sliced thin
2 small yellow squash, sliced thin
1/4 cup parsley, chopped
1 cup green onions, chopped
6 garlic cloves, chopped
1 cup sun-dried tomatoes, chopped
1/4 cup fresh basil, chopped
Salt and pepper

Dressing

1 lemon, zested
1/2 cup lemon juice
1/4 cup red wine vinegar
1/4 cup fresh basil, chopped
1 tablespoon dried basil
1 tablespoon Dijon mustard
1/2 tablespoon salt
3/4 teaspoon black pepper
1 1/2 cups olive oil
1/2 cup canola oil

1. Cook pasta, drain and cool. Reserve.

2. Cook green beans in boiling water about 3 minutes and quickly refresh them under cold water to stop further cooking. Drain and cool.

3. Whisk dressing ingredients together in a bowl until well mixed. Adjust seasoning to taste. Reserve.

4. When ready to assemble, mix all ingredients together.

5. Mix dressing into salad, using only as much as needed. If any dressing remains after mixing, refrigerate it for another use.

Broccoli Salad with Bacon and Onions

3 heads broccoli, cut into florets
1 cup raisins
3/4 cup sunflower seeds
1 cup green onions
1 1/2 teaspoons salt
1 teaspoon pepper
1/4 cup cider vinegar
1 pound bacon, cut into cubes
2 red onions, diced

Dressing

1/2 cup Dijon mustard
1/2 cup honey
1 cup cider vinegar
1 1/2 cups canola oil
1/2 cup olive oil

1. Place broccoli florets in a bowl (do not blanch). Grate the stems into the bowl.

2. Add raisins, sunflower seeds, onions, salt, pepper and cider vinegar.

3. Sauté bacon. When done, drain well.

4. In the same pan, saute onions until soft (8 to 10 minutes).

5. In separate container, combine dressing ingredients until smooth.

6. Add 1 to 1 1/2 cups dressing to salad ingredients. Toss well, add salt and pepper. Serve at room temperature. Don't use too much dressing (drain if necessary).

Garden Pasta Salad

1 pound pasta, cooked
2 heads broccoli, cut into florets
3 carrots, thinly sliced
1 cup cherry tomatoes, halved
1 yellow squash, split in half lengthwise, sliced thin
1 zucchini, split in half lengthwise, sliced thin
1 cup green onions, sliced thin
1/2 cup parsley
1 tablespoon salt
2 teaspoons pepper
1/4 cup sesame seeds, toasted

1. Cook pasta, drain, cool. Reserve.

2. Blanch carrots and broccoli. Drain, rinse under cold water to stop vegetables from cooking.

3. Prepare all other ingredients and combine.

4. Mix well, add dressing. Add salt and pepper to taste.

Dressing

1 cup wheat germ, processed until fine
6 cloves garlic, chopped
1/2 cup soy sauce
1/4 cup sesame oil
1 1/2 cups lemon juice
2 cups canola oil
1 teaspoon salt
1 teaspoon pepper

1. Process wheat germ, garlic, lemon juice and soy sauce.

2. Add sesame and canola oils. Add salt and pepper. Mix until well combined.

This dressing is best if made a day in advance. It will thicken overnight. Simply add a small amount of water and/or lemon juice to thin down for a more "creamy" consistency.

Thai Noodle Salad with Vegetables and Spicy Peanut Sauce

1 pound udon noodles (thick, round fresh Japanese wheat noodles)
   or spaghetti
6 cups romaine lettuce, thinly sliced
4 cups green cabbage, thinly sliced
2 cups sweet potato, uncooked, peeled, grated
2 red bell peppers, julienned
2 green bell peppers, julienned
1 cup carrot, peeled, grated
1 cup bean sprouts
Fresh basil leaves, cilantro sprigs and mint sprigs for garnish (optional)

Spicy Peanut Sauce

2 tablespoons gingerroot, peeled, minced
1 1/2 tablespoons water
1 1/2 tablespoons soy sauce
1 cup creamy peanut butter
1/4 cup honey
1 tablespoon chili paste
6 garlic cloves, minced
4 limes, juiced

1. Combine all peanut sauce ingredients in a small bowl, stir well with a wire whisk. Reserve.

2. Cook noodles in boiling water for 3 minutes (omit seasoning packet, if included). Drain, rinse under cold water, and set aside. Follow manufacturer's directions on other types of noodles.

3. Combine lettuce and cabbage in a large bowl; toss well. Spread lettuce mixture over a large platter.

4. Place noodles in center of platter on top of lettuce mixture.

5. Arrange potato, red bell pepper, green bell pepper, carrot, and bean sprouts around noodles in individual mounds over lettuce mixture.

6. Drizzle Spicy Peanut Sauce over salad. Garnish with basil, cilantro and mint, if desired.

[Yield: 12 servings as side dish, 6 servings as entree]

Tomato, Broccoli and Pasta Salad

1 pound pasta, cooked, rinsed
3 heads broccoli, cut into florets
10 to 12 Roma tomatoes, cut in thin wedges
1 red onion, cut in strips
1/2 cup fresh basil, chopped
1/2 cup parsley, chopped

Dressing

1/2 cup sun-dried tomatoes
4 cloves garlic
3/4 cup red wine vinegar
4 tablespoons Balsamic vinegar
2 cups olive oil
1 teaspoon salt
1 teaspoon pepper

1. To make dressing: Mince garlic and tomatoes in processor. Add vinegars, salt, pepper. Add oil slowly and combine well. Reserve.

2. Prepare all salad ingredients and toss together in large mixing bowl.

3. Add dressing, mix well.

This salad is best to make within a couple of hours of serving to prevent broccoli from dissolving.

Antipasto

1 head cauliflower, cut in florets, blanched
5 carrots, sliced thin, blanched
4 zucchini, halved, sliced
2 green peppers, chopped in large pieces
2 red peppers, chopped in large pieces
1 cup green olives, whole
1 cup black olives, whole (preferably Kalamata)
1 cup pepperoncini (no stems)
1/2 red onion, julienned
1/2 cup parsley, chopped
1 1/2 cups celery, chopped

Dressing

8 cloves garlic, chopped
3 cups olive oil
1 cup red wine vinegar
1 teaspoon red pepper flakes
2 teaspoons fresh oregano (1 teaspoon dried)
Salt and pepper to taste

1. Combine vegetables in salad bowl. Reserve.

2. Whisk dressing ingredients together in separate bowl.

3. Pour dressing over vegetables, toss well. Adjust salt and pepper. Let stand 1 hour before serving.

Can substitute other vegetables of choice.

Chicken "Club" Salad

1/2 pound bacon, chopped, cooked crisp
8 cups chicken breast, boned, cut into bite-sized pieces
2 cups cherry tomatoes, halved
1/2 cup sliced green onions
1 1/2 cups celery, chopped

Basil Mayonnaise

4 cups mayonnaise
1/2 cup cider vinegar
Salt and pepper
1 cup fresh basil, chopped

1. Process Basil Mayonnaise ingredients until well combined and mixture is a pale green.

2. Toss salad with Basil Mayonnaise. Serve over bed of lettuce and garnish with croutons and a fresh basil leaf.

Cajun Catfish Sandwich with Rémoulade Sauce

6 to 8 catfish fillets, checked over for bones
Seasoned butter
6 to 8 Cornmeal Rolls (recipe in Dessert & Pastry section)
Lettuce, sliced red onion rings, tomato slices

Cajun Seasoning

2 tablespoons black pepper
1 tablespoon white pepper
1 tablespoon cayenne pepper
1 tablespoon thyme
1 tablespoon oregano
2 tablespoons salt
2 tablespoons paprika

Rémoulade Sauce

3 cups mayonnaise
3 tablespoons Dijon mustard
4 tablespoons cornichons, chopped
4 tablespoons capers, drained
4 tablespoons parsley, chopped
4 tablespoons fresh tarragon, chopped
2 anchovy fillets, optional

1. Combine all Rémoulade Sauce ingredients in processor. Blend until smooth. Allow to mellow overnight in refrigerator.

2. Mix Cajun Seasoning ingredients thoroughly and store in a jar.

3. Season catfish with Cajun Seasoning and sauté over high heat until browned but still holding together. Reserve and keep warm.

4. Split and toast bun.

3. Spread Rémoulade Sauce on bottom of soft bun. Add lettuce, catfish and sliced red onion. Place some Remoulade Sauce on top and replace top of bun. Serve with tomato slices on side.

(Yield: 6 to 8 servings)

Pesto Chicken-Cheese Sandwiches

1 large red bell pepper
4 boneless skinless chicken breast halves (about 1 1/2 pounds)
1 cup purchased pesto sauce, divided
2 tablespoons olive oil
2 tablespoons unsalted butter, room temperature
2 garlic cloves, minced
4 large country-style bread slices
1/2 pound Fontina cheese, sliced

1. Char pepper over gas flame or under broiler until blackened on all sides. Place pepper in paper bag and cool 10 minutes. Peel and core pepper. Cut into matchstick-sized strips.

2. Combine chicken and 2/3 cup pesto in shallow dish. Marinate 1 hour in refrigerator, turning occasionally.

3. Heat heavy large skillet over medium heat. Add chicken and cook until light brown and cooked through, about 5 minutes per side. Transfer to work surface; cover with foil and let rest 5 minutes. Cut chicken diagonally into thin slices. Season with salt and pepper.

4. Preheat broiler. Whisk together oil, butter and garlic in bowl. Season with salt and pepper. Spread mixture evenly over 1 side of each bread slice. Place bread slices, garlic side up, on broiler-proof pan. Boil until garlic mixture bubbles and is golden, about 1 minute. Spread remaining 1/3 cup pesto over bread slices. Top with chicken, then roasted peppers. Divide cheese evenly among sandwiches. Broil until cheese melts, about 3 minutes.

(Yield: 4 servings)

Hint

A good quality Mozzarella, Swiss, Brie or any cheese of your choice could be substituted.

Grilled Ham and Fresh Pineapple Sandwich

1 pound (16 ounces) ham, sliced thin
8 slices fresh pineapple, cut into rings
8 ounces Monterey Jack cheese, sliced or grated
Lettuce for garnish
1 red onion, sliced
4 Cornmeal Rolls (recipe in pastry section) or sourdough rolls

Lemon Mayonnaise

1 cup mayonnaise
1/2 cup sour cream
2 lemons juiced, zested
1 teaspoon salt
1 teaspoon pepper
1 tablespoon Dijon mustard

1. Grill ham and fresh pineapple in skillet.

2. Top 4 ounces grilled ham with 2 ounces cheese and let melt. Top with 2 slices pineapple. Reserve.

3. Combine Lemon Mayonnaise ingredients.

3. Serve ham and cheese on roll with Lemon Mayonnaise, lettuce and sliced red onion.

(Yield: 4 sandwiches)

Hint

Do yourself a favor and use fresh pineapple. Cut off top and bottom of pineapple, and then outer layer. Then slice into rings, removing woody center of pineapple ring. Discard center. Wrap leftover pineapple and keep in refrigerator for another use.

Grilled Smoked Turkey Sandwich

2 yellow onions, halved, sliced thin
8 slices sourdough bread
16 ounces cooked turkey, sliced thin
4 ounces Cheddar or Monterey Jack cheese, sliced or grated
Butter for grilling

Dressing

1 cup mayonnaise
1/2 cup sour cream
1/4 cup Dijon mustard
1/2 cup green onions, chopped
2 tablespoons parsley, chopped
2 tablespoons basil, chopped
1 teaspoon salt
1/2 teaspoon pepper
2 to 3 garlic cloves, chopped
1 lemon, juiced

1. Sauté onions until caramelized (see Glossary).

2. Prepare Dressing: combine all dressing ingredients and mix well.

3. For sandwich: Use a griddle or skillet. Spread dressing on one side of a slice of bread. Place 4 ounces turkey, 1 ounce cheese, and 2 ounces of caramelized onions on one half. Top with a second slice of bread. Grill on medium heat until golden brown. Turn over and cook until cheese is melted and bread is golden brown. Remove from griddle and keep warm. May need to do in batches. Serve with dill pickle spears.

(Yield: 4 servings)

Bar-B-Que Chicken Breast Sandwich

8 chicken breast halves, boneless, skinless, thawed
10 strips bacon, cooked, chopped
2 tomatoes, sliced
1/2 cup green onions, chopped
8 ounces Cheddar cheese, sliced or grated
8 sandwich buns

Bar-B-Que Sauce

1 cup cider vinegar
2 tablespoons fresh ginger, grated
2 tablespoons dry mustard
2 cups ketchup
2 tablespoons Worchestershire sauce
2 garlic cloves, crushed, left whole
1 cup brown sugar
1 lemon, sliced
1 lemon, juiced
2 teaspoons salt
3 ounces whole butter

1. Put all sauce ingredients except butter in a thick-bottomed pot. Bring to boil, reduce heat, simmer for 15 minutes.

2. Add butter. Whisk until butter is dissolved. Take off heat. Throw lemon slices away. Strain remainder, pushing through sieve. Reserve. This makes enough sauce for several uses and will keep well for quite a while refrigerated or frozen.

3. Place chicken breasts in bowl, coat with 1 cup Bar-B-Que sauce. Mix well. Make sure chicken is well coated. Place in casserole dish or greased baking sheet. Spread more sauce on top.

4. Bake 8 to 10 minutes at 350 degrees until done. Do not overcook. Keep warm.

5. On each breast, place chopped bacon, tomato, green onion, more sauce and Cheddar cheese. Melt under broiler.

6. Serve on bun with lettuce and more tomato.

(Yield: 8 sandwiches)

Grilled Roast Beef and Cheese Sandwich on Cornmeal Roll

4 Cornmeal Rolls, split, toasted (recipe in pastry section)
16 ounces uncooked roast beef, thinly sliced
2 onions, caramelized (see Glossary)
8 ounces sliced cheese (Swiss, Provolone or Brie)

Horseradish Mayonnaise

1 cup mayonnaise
3 garlic cloves, chopped
1/2 cup sour cream
1/4 cup Dijon mustard
2 tablespoons prepared horseradish
Salt, black pepper

1. Grill beef, onions, salt, pepper until hot and top with sliced cheese.

2. Split and toast bun.

3. Process Horseradish Mayonnaise ingredients.

4. Spread Horseradish Mayonnaise on a bun. Top with beef and cheese.

(Yield: 4 sandwiches)

Vegetable Bowtie Pasta with Fresh Asparagus

1 pound bowtie pasta (farfalle)
1 pound butter
2 lemons, zested, juiced
1 teaspoon salt
1 teaspoon pepper
1 cup almonds, chopped
1 pound asparagus, cut in 2-inch pieces, blanched, cooled
2 fresh tomatoes, seeded, chopped
1 cup fresh Parmesan cheese

1. Cook pasta. Cool, toss with oil to prevent sticking.

2. Melt butter. Add lemon juice and zest, salt, pepper and almonds. Mix well, keep warm.

3. Combine pasta, asparagus, tomatoes, Parmesan cheese, salt and pepper to taste.

4. Pour butter mixture over pasta mixture and toss to combine. Add the butter in batches, as you may not need it all. Keep in refrigerator for 2 to 3 days.

(Yield: 6 to 8 servings)

125

Vegetarian Pizza

8 6-inch pizza shells, baked
Toasted Almond Pesto
2 onions, sliced thin, caramelized
2 bell peppers, julienned, sautéed with garlic
1 head broccoli, cut into florets, blanched
8 Roma tomatoes, sliced
3/4 cup black olives, sliced
1/4 cup fresh basil, chopped
4 cups Mozzarella cheese, grated
2 cups Parmesan cheese

Toasted Almond Pesto

10 garlic cloves
2 cups almonds, toasted
1/4 cup white wine
1 1/2 cups olive oil
2 tablespoons cayenne
2 tablespoons paprika
1 teaspoon salt

1. Process Toasted Almond Pesto ingredients. Reserve.

2. Spread pizza shells with Toasted Almond Pesto, and then other ingredients, adding cheeses last.

3. Bake slightly at 350 degrees for 5 to 7 minutes, or until cheese has melted.

(Yield: 8 6-inch pizzas)

Pasta with Peppers, Walnuts and Gorgonzola

Pasta Mixture

1 cup frozen peas, thawed
1 pound rotelle pasta, cooked, warm
2 red bell peppers, julienned, sautéed until tender
1 cup walnuts, toasted
1/2 cup Parmesan cheese, grated
2 cups Gorganzola cheese, crumbled (about 8 ounces)
Salt and pepper

Walnut Sauce

3 garlic cloves
1 cup walnuts
1/2 cup Parmesan cheese
1/2 teaspoon salt
1/2 teaspoon pepper
3/4 cup olive oil
2 tablespoons red wine vinegar

1. Combine pasta mixture ingredients, except for cheeses. Reserve.

2. Combine walnut sauce ingredients in food processor and process well. If mixture is too thick, thin to desired consistency with water. Adjust salt and pepper.

3. Toss pasta mixture with cheeses to melt the cheese.

4. Add walnut sauce. Mix well.

(Yield: 6 to 8 servings)

Hint

Use a good quality, authentic Gorgonzola. You can substitute almonds if desired.

Pasta with Artichokes and Mushrooms

4 1/2 cups artichokes, quartered, frozen or may substitute
   canned, well drained
1 1/2 cups strong brewed coffee
1 1/2 cups cream
3 tablespoons Dijon mustard
1 1/2 teaspoons fresh rosemary, chopped
Salt and pepper
3 tablespoons olive oil
3/4 pound mushrooms, sliced
Parmesan cheese
2 pounds fresh or dry fettuccini

1. Marinate the artichokes in the coffee for 15 minutes.

2. Stir in the cream and bring to a boil. Reduce the heat to
   moderately low and simmer until the liquid is reduced by one
   fourth, about 10 minutes.

3. Blend in the mustard and rosemary and season with salt and
   pepper to taste.

4. Meanwhile, heat the olive oil in the skillet and sauté
   mushrooms until lightly browned. Set aside.

5. Cook pasta al dente, drain and toss with oil. Reheat in water
   bath. Toss drained pasta with sauce and artichokes and
   Parmesan cheese and top with mushrooms.

(Yield: 10 to 12 servings)

Ricotta Gnocchi with Marinara Sauce and Pesto

1 egg
2 teaspoons salt
2 cups Ricotta cheese
1 1/2 to 2 cups flour, plus additional flour for preparation
2 tablespoons olive oil
3 cups prepared Marinara sauce
Prepared pesto (about 1/2 cup)
1 1/2 cups Parmesan cheese

1. Assemble Gnocchi: beat egg in large bowl, add salt, ricotta and 1 1/2 cups flour. Mix with a plastic spatula. Combine until a dough is formed. If the dough is sticky, add additional flour.

2. Bring a large pot of water to the boil. Add olive oil and salt. Turn off, keep reserved until ready to cook Gnocchi, then bring back to the boil.

3. Take a small portion of dough, about size of fist, and place on lightly floured surface. Roll dough into ropes with palms of hands until about 1-inch thick. Cut into 2-inch long pieces. Place on lightly floured tray and reserve. Continue rolling until all dough is used. These can be made ahead, kept wrapped in the refrigerator.

4. Bring water to boil, add Gnocchi, and stir. The Gnocchi will sink to the bottom. Wait about 1 minute and the Gnocchi will start to rise back to the surface of the water. Wait until all Gnocchi is floating on top. Be sure to stir the bottom to release any that may have stuck.

5. Drain through a colander, toss with heated Marinara sauce and 1 cup of Parmesan cheese. Top with remaining cheese and pesto.

(Yield: 6 to 8 servings)

Hint

Use a good quality purchased Marinara sauce and pesto sauce. This is much simpler than preparing from scratch.

Mushroom Stroganoff

8 garlic cloves, chopped
2 yellow onions, diced
2 pounds button mushrooms, sliced
1 tablespoon thyme
2 teaspoons tarragon
1 teaspoon salt
1 teaspoon pepper
1/2 cup sherry
1/4 cup Worcestershire sauce
1 cup vegetable stock
3 cups sour cream
1/2 cup Dijon mustard
Dashes of Tabasco
1 pound egg noodles, cooked

1. Sauté garlic and onions.

2. Add button mushrooms and cook 5 minutes until tender.

3. Add thyme, tarragon, salt and pepper. Mix well.

4. Add sherry, Worcestershire sauce and vegetable stock. Simmer, reduce until most of the liquid is gone.

5. Mix in sour cream and Dijon mustard.

6. Serve over cooked and drained egg noodles.

(Yield: 8 to 10 servings)

Pizza Primavera

8 6-inch pizza shells, baked, but not crisp
2 garlic cloves, chopped
1 zucchini, sliced thin
1 yellow squash, sliced thin
1 pound mushrooms, sliced
1 head broccoli, cut into florets, blanched
10 Roma tomatoes, sliced thin
1 cup black olives, chopped or sliced
4 cups Monterey Jack cheese, grated
1 cup Parmesan cheese, grated

Tomato Sauce

3 tablespoons olive oil
4 garlic cloves, chopped
1 1/2 yellow onions, chopped roughly
4 cups canned diced tomatoes, drained
3 tablespoons tomato paste
1 cup sun-dried tomatoes, chopped
1 tablespoon dried oregano
2 teaspoons dried thyme
2 teaspoons dried basil
2 teaspoons salt
1 bay leaf
1/4 cup fresh basil, chopped

1. Prepare Tomato Sauce: Sauté garlic and onions in olive oil until tender, about 10 minutes. Stir constantly to prevent garlic from burning. Add all remaining sauce ingredients. Bring to simmer and continue cooking about 45 minutes to 1 hour. Cool slightly. Discard bay leaf. Puree in batches until smooth. Adjust salt and pepper to taste. Reserve.
2. Sauté garlic, zucchini and yellow squash until tender. Reserve.
3. Sauté mushrooms until tender. Reserve.
4. Assemble: spread shells with Tomato Sauce, top with small amounts of the remaining ingredients, with cheeses on top.
5. Place on baking sheet, bake in a 350 degree oven about 7 to 10 minutes or until fully heated and cheese is melted. Sprinkle some additional Parmesan cheese on top after pizzas are removed from the oven.

Almond Chicken Salad Sandwiches

One of our most popular items.

4 cups celery, roughly chopped
1 cup stuffed green olives
1 cup almonds, toasted
8 cups chicken, cooked, cubed
1/2 cup green onions, chopped
1/4 cup parsley, chopped
2 teaspoons salt
1 teaspoon black pepper
3 1/2 cups mayonnaise
1 lemon, juiced

1. Using a processor, coarsely chop celery, olives, almonds and chicken. This will take several small batches. Mix together in a large bowl.

2. Add remaining ingredients and mix well. Adjust salt and pepper to taste.

3. Serve as a sandwich spread. Best if served on a fresh baked croissant, spread with additional mayonnaise and lettuce.

(Yield: 12 to 15 sandwiches)

Hint

This makes abut 3 quarts. Salad will keep in refrigerator 3 to 5 days or cut recipe in half if desired.

Notes

Notes

Wild Rice-Mushroom Soup

5 garlic cloves
3 yellow onions, diced
5 carrots, cut in small chunks
1/2 bunch celery
3 pounds mushrooms, sliced
1 bay leaf
1 tablespoon thyme
1 tablespoon salt
1 1/2 teaspoons black pepper
1 1/2 teaspoons white pepper
1/4 teaspoon cayenne pepper
1/4 teaspoon rubbed sage
2 tablespoons Worcestershire sauce
1 gallon vegetable stock
3 cups wild rice, cooked

1. Mince garlic in food processor. Reserve.

2. Pulse onions, carrots and celery separately (not too fine). Reserve.

3. Sauté garlic and onions in large saucepan.

4. Add carrots, celery and mushrooms, cook until everything is soft.

5. Add remaining ingredients except rice. Add just enough stock to cover vegetables, bring to a boil. Reduce heat and simmer 15 minutes. Stir in rice.

Creole Jambalaya

1/2 pound ham, cut in 1-inch pieces
2 onions, chopped
4 garlic cloves, chopped
1/2 cup parsley, chopped
2 tablespoons butter
4 cups chicken meat, cooked, cut in bite size pieces
1/2 teaspoon thyme
2 bay leaves
1/4 teaspoon ground cloves
1/2 pound Italian sausage, cooked, cut into 1/2-inch pieces
2 cups water
3/4 cups rice
2 teaspoons paprika
4 teaspoons salt
Pepper to taste
1/2 teaspoon cayenne pepper
1 teaspoon Tabasco sauce

1. Process ham in processor until coarsely chopped, 8 to 10 pulses. Reserve.

2. Drop garlic into running machine and mince. Reserve.

3. In a heavy bottomed pot, melt butter and cook onions and garlic until onions are soft.

4. Add the chicken, ham, parsley, herbs, cloves and cook for 5 to 7 minutes, stirring often.

5. Add sausage and cook 5 minutes more.

6. Add water and when it comes to the boil, stir in rice, paprika, salt, pepper and cayenne pepper.

7. Cover and simmer for 20 minutes or just until rice is tender.

8. Add Tabasco to taste.

Variation

Cooked shrimp and other seafood may be added to the rice mixture during the last 5 minutes of cooking to make a seafood jambalaya.

Cream of Carrot and Lemon Soup

1 cup (2 sticks) butter
5 medium yellow onions
8 garlic cloves, chopped
8 cups carrots, peeled, sliced
3 cups canned diced tomatoes, drained
3 baking potatoes, peeled, sliced
2 tablespoons dried basil
1 gallon (16 cups) chicken or vegetable stock
1 tablespoon salt
1 1/2 teaspoons pepper
4 cups crème fraiche (see below)
1 teaspoon Tabasco sauce
1 cup lemon juice

Crème Fraiche

Gently whisk even portions of sour cream and heavy cream until consistency is smooth and easy to pour. May thicken upon standing. If so, stir in more cream until desired consistency.

1. In large saucepan, sauté onions and garlic in butter until tender.

2. Add carrots, tomatoes, potatoes, basil, stock and salt and pepper.

3. Bring to a boil, cover and cook 45 minutes.

4. Strain soup, reserve broth.

5. Puree vegetables.

6. Combine vegetable puree with broth, crème fraiche and Tabasco sauce.

(Yield: 10 to 12 servings)

Pumpkin Soup

4 yellow onions, chopped
1/2 cup (1 stick) butter
29-ounce can solid pack pumpkin
6 cups vegetable stock
2 tablespoons sugar
1/2 cup sherry

White Sauce

1 cup (2 sticks) butter
2 cups flour
1 1/2 gallons milk

1. Sauté onions in butter until translucent, do not brown!

2. Add pumpkin, stock, sugar and sherry to onions. Simmer for 15 to 20 minutes until mixture is smooth. Reserve.

3. For white sauce: Melt butter on low heat. Whisk in flour and salt, making sure to mix well and scrape bottom and sides of pan. Add milk in batches (2 cups at a time). Stir constantly, adding more milk as sauce thickens.

4. When all milk has been added to white sauce, cook approximately 3 to 5 minutes. Transfer white sauce to container to cool slightly.

5. Add white sauce to pumpkin puree.

6. Serve with a dollop of lightly salted whipped cream.

(Yield: 10 to 12 servings)

Italian Vegetable Soup

4 onions, chopped
5 garlic cloves, minced
2 pounds mushrooms, sliced
4 carrots, peeled, grated
4 cups tomatoes, diced
1 cup peas
2 cups white beans, cooked
12 to 16 cups vegetable stock
1/4 cup Worcestershire sauce
1/2 cup dry sherry
1 teaspoon crushed red pepper flakes
1/4 cup parsley, chopped
Salt and pepper to taste

1. Sauté onions and garlic in large saucepan.

2. Add mushrooms, cook until both onions and mushrooms are soft.

3. Stir in remaining ingredients.

4. Bring to boil, reduce heat. Simmer 30 minutes. Garnish with croutons and Parmesan cheese.

(Yield: 12 to 14 servings)

Lowfat Tuscan Ribollita

10 slices Italian bread, cut 1/4-inch thick
1 garlic clove, halved
2 tablespoons olive oil
1 large onion, halved, sliced
2 carrots, sliced
2 celery stalks, sliced
2 garlic cloves, minced
1 small zucchini, sliced
1/2 red bell pepper, diced
1/4 teaspoon dried rosemary, crumbled
2 cups canned tomatoes, drained, reserve juices
1 cup chicken stock or canned broth
2 tablespoons freshly grated Parmesan cheese

1. Preheat oven to 350 degrees.

2. Place bread on a small baking sheet. Bake until crisp and golden brown, about 15 minutes. Cool slightly.

3. Rub both sides of bread with halved garlic clove. Can be prepared 1 day ahead. Cover, store at room temperature.

4. Heat olive oil in heavy large skillet over medium heat.

5. Add onion and sauté until onion is tender, about 12 minutes.

6. Stir in carrots, celery and 2 minced garlic cloves.

7. Cover and cook until carrots are almost tender, stirring occasionally, about 10 minutes.

8. Add zucchini, red bell pepper and rosemary and sauté until the zucchini is almost crisp, tender, about 5 minutes.

9. Mix in drained tomatoes. Season to taste with salt and pepper.

10. Preheat oven to 400 degrees.

11. Place vegetable mixture into casserole dish. Arrange garlic toast in single layer atop vegetable mixture in casserole dish.

12. Pour broth and reserved juices from tomatoes over the toast.

13. Sprinkle with Parmesan cheese.

14. Bake until toast is moist and cheese is golden brown, about 30 minutes. Let stand for 5 minutes and serve.

(Yield: 10 to 12 servings)

Artichoke, Asparagus and Potato Stew with Mint

2 medium yellow onions, diced
2 to 3 leeks, washed, diced
1/2 bunch celery, chopped
10 red potatoes, sliced in half
6 cups vegetable stock
1 tablespoon thyme
1 tablespoon salt
1/2 cup mint, chopped
1/2 cup parsley, chopped
1 pound baby carrots, blanched 3 to 5 minutes
1 pound asparagus, cut in 1-inch pieces
2 cups artichoke hearts, chopped
1/4 cup lemon juice
Salt and pepper

1. Sauté onions, leeks and celery until soft.

2. Add potatoes, stock, thyme, salt, mint and parsley.

3. Simmer until potatoes are almost done, then add carrots, asparagus, artichoke hearts, lemon juice and salt and pepper to taste. Continue cooking until all vegetables are cooked.

(Yield: 10 to 12 servings)

Soups & Stews

Italian Vegetable Stew with Polenta

Polenta

8 cups water
1 tablespoon salt
2 cups polenta
1/2 cup (1 stick) whole butter, cut in small pieces
1 1/2 cups Parmesan cheese
1/2 cup fresh basil, chopped
1/4 cup fresh tarragon, chopped
Salt

1. Bring water and salt to a boil. Slowly stir in polenta.

2. Reduce heat, simmer for 5 minutes or so, until it starts to thicken.

3. Add butter, cheese, basil, tarragon and salt to taste.

4. Pour into greased 13-inch by 9-inch pan. Place foil directly on top. Let firm up in refrigerator overnight.

Italian Stew

3 carrots, sliced thin
1/2 bunch celery, chopped
5 to 6 garlic cloves, chopped
2 medium onions, chopped
1 1/2 zucchini, split in half, sliced thin
1 1/2 yellow squash, split in half, sliced thin
6 cups canned tomatoes, chopped
2 cups artichoke hearts
1 cup garbanzo beans, canned
2 teaspoon dried thyme
2 teaspoon dried basil
2 teaspoon dried oregano
2 bay leaves
Salt and pepper
1/2 pound fresh spinach, chopped
1/4 cup fresh basil, chopped
Parmesan cheese

1. Sauté carrots, celery, garlic, onions, zucchini and squash.

2. Add tomatoes, artichoke hearts and garbanzo beans.

3. Add thyme, basil, oregano, bay leaves, salt and pepper.

4. Simmer for 15 to 20 minutes. Add spinach and basil

5. To serve: Heat polenta. Cut polenta in triangles. Place 3 triangles in a bowl, cover with stew. Top with Parmesan cheese. Make sure polenta is hot.

(Yield: 12 to 14 servings)

Three Bean Stew

1 cup white beans (Great Northern)
1 cup black beans
1 cup kidney beans
4 to 5 garlic cloves
5 medium onions
1 red bell pepper, diced
1 green bell pepper, diced
1/2 bunch celery, chopped
2 carrots, cut into 1/2-inch pieces
1 1/2 zucchini, cut into 1/2-inch slices
6 cups diced tomatoes
1 tablespoon curry
1 tablespoon cumin
1 tablespoon basil
1 tablespoon coriander
1 tablespoon oregano
Salt and pepper
Vegetable stock

1. Soak, cook beans until tender. Cool.

2. Sauté garlic, onions, peppers, celery, carrots and zucchini. When all are tender, add tomatoes, spices, stock and salt and pepper to taste.

3. Add beans. Simmer 15 to 20 minutes.

4. Puree 2 to 3 cups of bean mixture, pour back into stew. You want it to be thick.

5. Top with salsa, green onions.

(Yield: 10 to 12 servings)

Carrot and Chestnut Soup

1/2 pound fresh chestnuts **or**
   1/2 cup canned unsweetened chestnut puree
2 yellow onions, coarsely chopped
2 pounds carrots, sliced crosswise 1/2-inch thick
1 cup celery, thinly sliced crosswise
1 tablespoon fresh ginger, finely chopped
8 cups vegetable stock
Salt and freshly ground pepper
Chopped fresh chives

1. If using fresh chestnuts, preheat the oven to 400 degrees. Cut an X on the flat side of each chestnut. Roast them on a small baking sheet for 15 minutes. Let cool, then peel.

2. In a large saucepan, simmer the onion with 1/4 cup of water stirring until softened, 7 to 8 minutes.

3. Add carrots, celery, ginger, vegetable stock and chestnuts to the saucepan. Simmer over moderate heat until the carrots are tender (about 25 minutes).

4. In a blender, puree the soup in batches until smooth. Transfer to a warm soup tureen. Season with salt and pepper, garnish with chives and serve.

(Yield: 10 servings)

Garlic Soup

2 yellow onions, cut in half, sliced
2 cups garlic cloves, chopped
1 1/2 to 2 loaves stale French bread
2 Idaho potatoes, cubed
1 1/2 teaspoons thyme
2 bay leaves
1/2 teaspoon grated nutmeg
Salt and pepper
4 cups vegetable stock
1/2 cup cream
Croutons
Parmesan cheese

1. Sauté onions until tender (8 to 10 minutes).

2. Add garlic, stirring constantly to caramelize onions with garlic.

3. When onions and garlic are very soft, add bread, potatoes, thyme, bay leaves, nutmeg and salt and pepper to taste. Mix well.

4. Cover with vegetable stock and simmer for 20 to 30 minutes.

5. Puree mixture (should be thick).

6. To serve, add cream and salt and pepper to taste. Serve topped with croutons and Parmesan cheese.

(Yield: 10 servings)

New Mexico Green Chile Pork Stew

1 pound tomatillos
1 tablespoon salt
2 1/2 pounds pork stew meat
Flour, for dredging meat
7 medium yellow onions, diced
1 1/2 cups green chilies, chopped
1 tablespoon cumin
1 1/2 teaspoons chili powder
1 1/2 teaspoons salt
1 1/2 teaspoons oregano
2 to 3 cups chicken stock
1/2 cup fresh cilantro, chopped
1 lemon, juiced
2 teaspoons salt
1 teaspoon pepper

1. Place tomatillos in stockpot, cover with water and add salt. Bring to a boil and boil for 5 minutes. Drain. Cool.

2. Process to "chunky". Reserve.

3. Dredge meat in flour and brown. Reserve.

4. Sauté garlic, onion, green chilies, cumin, chili powder, salt and oregano 5 to 10 minutes.

5. Add chicken stock and simmer for 5 minutes.

6. Add browned meat and tomatillo mixture (add more stock if necessary, should be thick).

7. Simmer 30 to 45 minutes until meat is tender, stirring regularly to avoid scorching.

8. Adjust seasonings (may need to add sugar if tomatillo mixture is too sour) and add cilantro, lemon juice and salt and pepper to taste before serving.

(Yield: 12 to 14 servings)

Butternut Squash and Apple Soup

7 yellow onions, chopped
6 pounds butternut squash, peeled, seeded, cubed (about 3 large)
2 to 3 Idaho potatoes, peeled, cubed
2 pounds Granny Smith apples, peeled, sliced
1 1/2 teaspoons nutmeg, freshly-grated
1 teaspoon ground cloves
1 1/2 teaspoon thyme
1 1/2 teaspoon cinnamon
2 bay leaves
Salt and pepper
Sour cream

1. Sauté onions

2. Add squash, potatoes, apples and seasonings.

3. Cover with vegetable stock by 3 inches. Simmer for 30 minutes.

4. Cool slightly.

5. Puree. Salt and pepper to taste.

6. When serving, thin with cream. Garnish with sour cream and nutmeg.

(Yield: 12 to 14 servings)

Autumn Beef Stew

2 1/2 pounds beef, cut in 1 1/2-inch cubes
2 cups red wine, Burgundy
2 tablespoons cumin
4 garlic cloves, minced
1 orange, zested
1 butternut squash, peeled, seeded, cubed
2 medium onions, diced
2 cups celery, chopped
2 carrots, sliced thin
1 pound mushrooms, sliced
2 cups tomato juice
2 cups diced tomatoes, canned
1 tablespoon dried thyme
1 bay leaf
1 tablespoon salt
1 teaspoon pepper

1. Combine beef, wine, cumin, pepper, garlic and orange rind in a bowl.

2. Mix well, cover, refrigerate overnight.

2. Pat meat dry (reserve marinade). Sauté beef on all sides; remove and reserve.

4. In large stockpot, sauté onions, carrots, celery and mushrooms 3 to 5 minutes until tender.

5. Add squash, beef, tomatoes and tomato juice. Continue cooking approximately 5 minutes. Add reserved marinade, thyme, bay leaves, salt and pepper.

6. Bring to a boil; reduce heat, simmer 1 hour.

This stew is best if made in advance, allowed to thicken overnight and served the next day.

If stew becomes too thick, add water or more tomato juice. Also, some Worcestershire sauce and dashes of Tabasco add a nice touch to the stew.

Serve over egg noodles.

(Yield: 12 servings)

Sweet and Spicy Vegetable Stew

1 head cauliflower
1 pound green beans
5 garlic cloves, chopped
2 onions, diced
2 carrots, sliced thin
2 cups celery, chopped
1 red bell pepper, diced
1 green bell pepper, diced
4 cups canned diced tomatoes
2 teaspoons tumeric
2 teaspoons cinnamon
2 teaspoons ginger
2 teaspoons paprika
1 teaspoon salt
1 teaspoon pepper
1 teaspoon red pepper flakes
1 cup chopped prunes
1 cup garbanzo beans

1. Blanch cauliflower and green beans. Reserve.

2. Sauté garlic, onion, carrots, celery and peppers.

3. Add tomatoes, turmeric, cinnamon, ginger, paprika, salt, pepper and red pepper flakes. Simmer for 20 minutes.

4. Add prunes, garbanzo beans and blanched vegetables.

(Yield: 10 to 12 servings)

Hint

Serve over couscous in center of bowl.

Gingered Sweet Potato Soup

4 medium onions, diced
8 garlic cloves, chopped
4 tablespoons fresh ginger, peeled, roughly chopped
6 sweet potatoes, peeled, cubed
2 Idaho potatoes, peeled, cubed
2 bay leaves
1 1/2 teaspoons cinnamon
2 teaspoons nutmeg
1/2 teaspoon cloves
Lots of salt and pepper
8 to 12 cups vegetable stock
Cream

1. Sauté onions, garlic and ginger.

2. Add potatoes, bay leaves, cinnamon, nutmeg, cloves and salt and pepper to taste.

3. Mix well and add vegetable stock to cover (plus a little more).

4. Bring to a boil, then simmer for 1 hour. Cook until the potatoes are well done.

5. Puree mixture and adjust salt and pepper to taste. Add cream to thin to desired consistency.

(Yield: 12 to 14 servings)

Vegetarian Chili

1/3 cup olive oil
1 cup celery, chopped
1 cup carrots, chopped
2 cups mushrooms, chopped
1 tablespoon ground cumin
2 tablespoons chili powder
1 tablespoon salt
2 cups tomato juice
2 cups chopped tomatoes
1/2 teaspoon Tabasco
3 tablespoons tomato paste
1 cup canned green chilies or to taste, chopped
2 cups onionsm finely chopped
1 cup green peppers, chopped
1 tablespoon garlic, minced
1/4 teaspoon red pepper flakes
3/4 teaspoons dried oregano
1/2 teaspoon pepper
1 cup bulgur wheat
2 cups cooked kidney beans
2 lemons, juiced
1 tablespoon Worcestershire sauce

1. Have all of the ingredients ready.

2. Heat the olive oil in a large skillet. Over high heat, add the onions, celery, green peppers, carrots, garlic, mushrooms, spices, salt and pepper. Cook, stirring for 1 to 2 minutes.

3. Add the remaining ingredients. Bring to a boil, stirring. Reduce the heat and simmer for 20 minutes, uncovered. If too thick, the chili can be thinned with additional tomato juice.

(Yield: 2 quarts, 12 to 14 servings)

Tomato Bisque

Soup Base

2 to 3 medium yellow onions, finely minced in processor
12 cups canned, diced tomatoes (with juice)
2 tablespoons dried basil
1/2 cup brewed espresso, purchase or brew
2 tablespoon sugar
1 tablespoon salt
2 teaspoons white pepper

White Sauce

1 cup (2 sticks) butter
2 cups flour
1/2 gallon milk
2 tablespoons tomato paste

1. Sauté onions in butter in large pot until tender.
2. Process tomatoes in small batches until coarsely pureed. Add to sautéed onions.
3. Add remaining ingredients to onion mixture and simmer 10 to 15 minutes. Reserve.
4. For white sauce: melt butter on low-medium heat. Whisk in flour and salt, making sure to mix well and scrape the bottom of the pan with a rubber spatula. Mix until thick paste forms.
5. Add milk in batches (2 cups at a time). Stir constantly, continuing to scape bottom and sides of pan. Add more milk as sauce thickens.
6. When all milk has been added, cook approximately 3 to 5 minutes or until sauce slightly thickens. Transfer white sauce to container to cool slightly.
7. Add white sauce to tomato soup base. Adjust salt and pepper. (Do not be alarmed if the soup appears "curdled". Cool completely and soup will thicken.)
8. When serving, heat slowly and whisk constantly to prevent scorching. Add milk or cream to reach desired consistancy. Adjust salt and pepper to taste.
9. Serve, garnished with croutons.

153

Black Bean Soup

8 cups black beans, soaked in cold water for 2 to 3 hours, drained
3 yellow onions, chopped fine
6 carrots, chopped fine
10 cloves garlic, chopped
2 tablespoons cumin
2 tablespoons chili powder
1 tablespoon oregano
1 teaspoon cayenne pepper
2 bay leaves
2 lemons, juiced
2 limes, juiced
1 tablespoon salt
2 teaspoons pepper
Sour cream, garnish
Chopped tomatoes, garnish
Green onions, sliced, for garnish

1. Soak beans in cold water overnight.

2. Bring beans to a boil. A black foam or scum will appear on the surface; discard by removing with a large spoon or ladle. You may need to add more water. Make sure beans are covered.

3. After most of foam is removed, add onions, garlic, carrots, cumin, chili powder, oregano, cayenne and bay leaves. Mix well. Simmer approximately 1 1/2 hours or until beans are done. Check by pressing a few beans against inside of pan with a spoon. Beans should be totally soft.

4. Add lemon juice, lime juice, salt and pepper. Serve with garnishes.

(Yield: 8 to 10 servings)

Corn Tortilla Soup

20 corn tortillas, cut very thinly in 2-inch strips
Oil for deep frying
4 medium onions, chopped
2 red peppers, chopped
10 garlic cloves, thinly sliced
1 cup green chilies, chopped
2 tablespoons ground cumin
3/4 cup tequila
1 gallon rich chicken stock
4 cups poached chicken meat, optional
1/4 cup lime juice (about 3 limes)
6 cups diced tomatoes
2 fresh jalapeño chilies, seeded, minced

1. Fry tortilla strips in oil in pot. Remove and drain. Reserve

2   Cook onions until soft.

3. Add garlic, bell peppers, jalapeños, green chilies, and cumin and cook about 3 minutes, stripping frequently.

4. Add tequila and cook until almost evaporated.

5. Add chicken stock and 1/3 of the tortilla strips.

6. Add chicken (if using) and tomatoes and simmer for 30 minutes, or until vegetables and chicken are tender. Season with salt and pepper and lime juice. Cover and chill.

7. Skim fat from surface of soup. Bring soup to simmer. Garnish soup with tortilla strips, cilantro and jack cheese.

(Yield: ___ to ___ servings)

Notes

Al dente ("to the tooth")

To cook vegetables, pasta, etc., until they are still slightly "crunchy" to the bite but not under-done. Check vegetables or pasta periodically throughout cooking time.

Blanch

To drop food into boiling, salted water and heat until just cooked but still slightly "crunchy," not over-cooked. After blanching, drain food through a colander and rinse with cold water to stop it from cooking further.

Caramelize

In this book, we refer to this in terms of onions. This is caused by the water in the onions evaporating as the sugar remaining is cooked, giving the onions a "sweet" taste. Sauté diced, sliced onions in whole butter on low heat until golden brown, stirring constantly. Slow cook as the longer time that the onions are cooked, the sweeter they become.

Chop

To cut food into pieces which can range from "fine" chop to "coarse" chop in size.

Clarify

The process of eliminating solids from butter. Melt butter and remove milk solids that rise to the top. Strain butter through a fine sieve to trap any additional solids. The remaining clear butter will not burn and can be used under high heat in many cooking applications.

Cover

To cover, simply place meat, vegetables, etc., in appropriate container. Pour enough recommended liquids into container to cover contents by approximately 1 inch. This allows contents to move around freely when cooked.

Curdle

Some food items, such as cream sauces and soups, can separate if cooked using too much heat. A cottage cheese-like substance will appear on the surface. Also, curdling can occur when food spoils. In either case, the food must be discarded and prepared again using lower heat.

Deglazing

The process of removing solids that have stuck to the bottom of the pan during cooking by simply adding liquid (wine, stock, etc.) to a hot pan.

Dice

To cut into equal-sized small cubes, from 1/4 inch to 1/2 inch.

Dimple

When cooking rice, barley, etc., after most of the liquid has evaporated, the top surface of the cooked rice will form small holes, or dimples. This is when you remove it from the heat.

Dollop

Nothing more than a fancy way of saying "blob." Generally a rounded spoonful of a topping used to enhance presentation or flavor. We serve a dollop of sour cream on our quiche, for example.

Dredge

To coat food by covering with flour, bread crumbs, or liquid. Examples would be dredging chicken breasts in flour before sautéing or French toast in batter before cooking.

Emulsify

The process of adding liquids to other ingredients to form a sauce or dressing. For example, oil is added to eggs to create a thick mayonnaise or dressing; melted butter is added to eggs to create Hollandaise Sauce. The "fat" (oil or butter) must be added very slowly during preparation to allow it to incorporate together. After the sauce is thickened, a variety of ingredients can be added to create different flavors.

Florets

These are the tops of the buds or flower of the broccoli and cauliflower plant. Cut florets off of the central stalk, leaving a stem about 2 inches long. Cut florets into bite-sized pieces so they cook evenly and are easier to eat.

Garnish

To add decorative accompaniments to prepared food dishes.

Julienne

To cut into thin strips, ideally the size of match sticks.

Mince

To chop into very fine pieces, no bigger than 1/8 inch.

Poach

To cook food gently in simmering liquid that is not allowed to boil.

Reduce

To decrease the amount of liquid in sauces, soups, stews. Simmer on medium to high heat to evaporate excess water and thicken. This improves the flavor making it more concentrated.

Roast

To cook completely in a hot, dry oven.

Sauté

To cook by frying in a hot pan using a little oil or butter to help coat food and prevent it from sticking to the pan.

Thickening

Adding an ingredient to make a sauce, dressing, etc., have a thicker base. Examples would be adding white sauce to thicken pureed soups, cornstarch to thicken sauces, or eggs to thicken dressings.

Thinning

Adding liquid to a dressing, sauce, soup, stew, etc., to reach a desired consistency.

Toast

To brown by baking (nuts, seeds) or by placing food under direct heat (toast, croutons, etc.).

Zest

This is the outer layer of citrus fruit. Using a citrus zester, paring knife, or vegetable peeler, remove the outer layer being careful not to include any of the white "pith" underneath it which is very bitter. A citrus zester will make the job easier as it cuts the peel into thin strands. After peel is removed, chop very fine.

To assist you in achieving the best results with the recipes in Le Poulet Rouge Cookbook, the following *conseils du chef* are provided by author Tim Holley.

- Be sure to wash vegetables and fruits before using.

- Try to use average size fresh ingredients. We use medium-sized onion in all our recipes.

- Peel and mince garlic or ginger as fine as possible.

- Use fresh herbs if possible.

- Use *fresh* grated Parmesan cheese, not "processed."

- Be sure to zest citrus first, then juice. You can keep zested, reserved citrus in refrigerator. It will firm up on the outside but can be used for juice.

- Use only fresh, top quality ingredients. We use whole milk, heavy cream, real sour cream, and large sized eggs in all recipes. Also, a well-stocked kitchen is essential.

- Stock up on items such as diced tomatoes, canned chilies, dried pastas, prepared Marinara sauce, canned stocks, oils, vinegars and spices. These will all keep indefinitely and are used frequently.

- Dried pastas can be substituted if a desired type is not available. When cooking pasta, add olive oil to water to prevent pasta from sticking together. Also add a good amount of salt to the water. These both help to flavor the pasta.

- Before beginning preparation of a recipe, be sure to read all directions and have all ingredients ready before you begin. This will let you know if you need to purchase an ingredient or if you need to prepare one or more ingredients early. Also, have your equipment and utensils ready.

- When preparing salads, keep in mind that some vegetables release water and, over a period of time, can cause the salad to become soggy. Simply drain excess liquid off and gently remix your salad.

- Always pre-heat ovens. Most of the oven recipes in this book call for a 350 degree (Fahrenheit) temperature. Ovens do vary greatly, however, so you must keep a close watch on your oven. You may need to adjust heat, or cover items if necessary.

- Yellow medium onions, unless otherwise noted.

- When adding dressing to a salad, use only part of the dressing, mix well, and add more as needed. Unused salad dressings keep for a long time when refrigerated.

- Vegetables based on average sizes.

- Oven 350 degrees

Glossary of Terms & Helpful Hints

Glossary of Terms & Helpful Hints

ORDER FORM

Did you enjoy this cookbook?
Need a great gift for a friend or loved one?

Name_____

Address_____

City_____

State _____ Zip Code_____

____ copies of *Le Poulet Rouge Restaurant Cookbook* at $19.95 ea. $_____

Idaho residents add 5% sales tax $_____

Send 10% for shipping $_____

TOTAL $_____

Include check for total amount, or use credit card as indicated below:

☐ Visa   ☐ MasterCard   Credit Card No. _____

Signature _____ Expiration Date_____

To order by phone call:
1-800-358-1929
Quantity orders invited - Call for bulk pricing

To order by mail:
Make checks payable to:

LEGENDARY PUBLISHING COMPANY
P.O. Box 7706
Boise, Idaho 83707-1706
U.S.A.

Please photocopy form if additional forms are needed.

Glossary of Terms & Helpful Hints